NOW OR NEVER!

54th Massachusetts Infantry's War to End Slavery

RAY ANTHONY SHEPARD

All Union soldiers wore eagles on their buttons.

CALKINS CREEK

An Imprint of Highlights
Honesdale, Pennsylvania

To Kathleen, for her daily encouragement and patience

Text copyright © 2017 by Ray Anthony Shepard

Calkins Creek
An Imprint of Highlights
815 Church Street
Honesdale, Pennsylvania 18431

Printed in the United States of America
ISBN: 978-1-62979-340-5 (hc)
ISBN: 978-1- 62979-916-2 (e-book)

Library of Congress Control Number: 2017937779

First edition
The text of this book is set in Bodoni Egyptian Pro.
Design by Tim Gillner
10 9 8 7 6 5 4 3 2 1

MEN OF COLOR, TO ARMS! NOW OR NEVER!

—Frederick Douglass

Former slave, abolitionist, author,
and recruiter for the Fifty-Fourth

CONTENTS

MEN OF COLOR, TO ARMS! NOW OR NEVER!

This is our Golden Moment. The Government of the United States calls for every Able-Bodied Colored Man to enter the Army for the THREE YEARS' SERVICE, and join in fighting the Battles of Liberty and the Union. A new era is open to us. For generations we have suffered under the horrors of slavery, outrage and wrong; our manhood has been denied, our citizenship blotted out, our souls seared and burned, our spirits cowed and crushed, and the hopes of the future of our race involved in doubts and darkness. But now the whole aspect of our relations to the white race is changed. Now therefore is our most precious moment. Let us Rush to Arms! **Fail Now and Our Race is Doomed** on this the soil of our birth. We must now awake, arise, or be forever fallen. If we value Liberty, if we wish to be free in this land, if we love our country, if we love our families, our children, our homes, we must strike NOW while the Country calls: must rise up in the dignity of our manhood, and show by our own right arms that we are worthy to be freemen. Our enemies have made the country believe that we are craven cowards, without soul, without manhood, without the spirit of soldiers. Shall we die with this stigma resting on our graves? Shall we leave this inheritance of shame to our children? No! A thousand times No! **We WILL Rise!** The alternative is upon us; let us rather die freemen than live to be slaves. What is life without liberty? We say that we have manhood—now is the time to prove it. A nation or a people that cannot fight may be pitied, but cannot be respected. If we would be regarded *Men*, if we would forever **SILENCE THE TONGUE OF CALUMNY,** of prejudice and hate; let us rise NOW and fly to arms! We have seen what **Valor and Heroism** our brothers displayed at **PORT HUDSON and at MILLIKEN'S BEND;** though they are just from the galling, poisoning grasp of slavery, they have startled the world by the most exalted heroism. If they have proved themselves heroes, can not we prove ourselves men? **ARE FREEMEN LESS BRAVE THAN SLAVES?** More than a Million White Men have left Comfortable Homes and joined the Armies of the Union to save their Country; cannot we leave ours, and swell the hosts of the Union, to save our liberties, vindicate our manhood, and deserve well of our Country?

MEN OF COLOR! All Races of Men—the Englishman, the Irishman, the Frenchman, the German, the American, have been called to assert their claim to freedom and a manly character, by an appeal to the sword. The day that has seen an enslaved race in arms, has, in all history, seen their last trial. We can now see that **OUR LAST OPPORTUNITY HAS COME!** If we are not lower in the scale of humanity than Englishmen, Irishmen, white Americans and other races, we can show it now.

MEN OF COLOR! BROTHERS and FATHERS! WE APPEAL TO YOU! By all your concern for yourselves and your liberties, by all your regard for God and Humanity, by all your desire for Citizenship and Equality before the law, by all your love for the Country, to stop at no subterfuges, listen to nothing that shall deter you from rallying for the Army. Come forward, and at once Enroll your Names for the **Three Years' Service.** **STRIKE NOW,** and you are henceforth and forever **FREEMEN!**

E. D. Bassett,	John W. Price,	Rev. J. Boulden,	John P. Burr,	Jas. R. Gordon,
Wm. D. Forten,	Augustus Dorsey,	Rev. J. Asher,	Robert Jones,	Samuel Stewart,
Frederick Douglass,	Rev. Stephen Smith,	Rev. J. C. Gibbs,	O. V. Catto,	David B. Bowser,
Wm. Whipper,	N. W. Depee,	Daniel George,	Thos. J. Dorsey,	Henry Minton,
D. D. Turner,	Dr. J. H. Wilson,	Robert M. Adger,	I. D. Cliff,	Daniel Colley,
Jas. McCrummell,	J. W. Cassey,	Henry M. Cropper,	Jacob C. White,	J. C. White, Jr.,
A. S. Cassey,	P. J. Armstrong,	Rev. J. B. Reeve,	Morris Hall,	Rev. J. P. Campbell,
A. M. Green,	J. W. Simpson,	Rev. J. A. Williams,	James Needham,	Rev. W. J. Alston,
J. W. Page,	Rev. J B. Trusty,	Rev. A. L. Stanford,	Rev. Elisha Weaver,	J. P. Johnson,
L. R. Seymour,	S. Morgan Smith,	Thomas J. Bowers,	Ebenezer Black,	Franklin Turner,
Rev. J. Underdue,	Wm. E. Gipson,	Elijah J. Davis,	Rev. Wm. T. Catto,	Jesse E. Glasgow.

Throughout this story I have retained the word "nigger" as found in contemporary letters and newspaper articles written by Whites and Blacks in the 1860s. This offensive word gives readers a better understanding of the social and political challenges faced by Americans of African descent before, during, and for many years after the Civil War. The use of this spiteful word today is rude, hurtful, and disruptive, regardless of the speaker's racial identity.

Also please note I have chosen to capitalize Black and White when writing about a group or race of people.

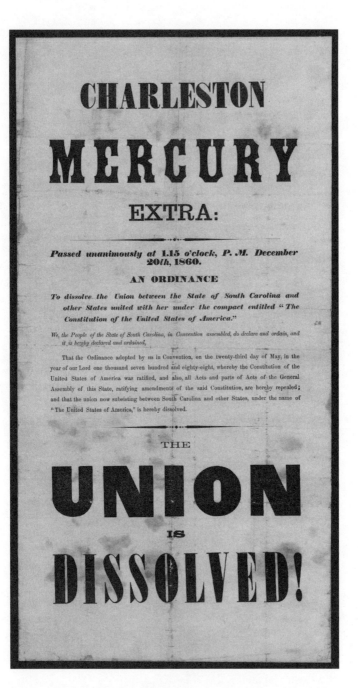

Notice of South Carolina's secession on December 20, 1860, two months before Lincoln became president.

CHAPTER ONE
GEORGE E. STEPHENS

Abraham Lincoln's election meant war, a war of the worst kind, a civil war. By the time Lincoln spoke his first word as president, seven states had declared their independence and formed the Confederate States of America. More states would follow. Some African Americans in the North saw it as a time of promise. The secession of slave states meant a chance to get their hands around the "throat of treason and slavery."

On the muggy morning of March 21, 1861, three weeks after Lincoln's inauguration, the streets in Savannah, Georgia, overflowed in raucous celebration. Soldiers in regiments nicknamed the Rattlesnakes and the Hyenas paraded for cheering citizens. Boisterous men, with visions of a kingdom of wealth forced from the sweat of generations of Black slave laborers, carried a large crude drawing. It showed a ripped and tattered Stars and Stripes, hanging by threads from a broken staff. An open grave waited below the flag. Scrawled in large letters:

"RECEIVE ME."

From 1771 to 1856, thousands of slaves were sold in front of this building, the Charleston Custom House. Slave traders called their lucrative business "black ivory." The Declaration of Independence was read aloud to the people of Charleston from one of the balconies in 1776, and George Washington met here with Charleston's citizens in 1791.

The crowds pressed their way to a large meeting hall. They wanted to hear Alexander Hamilton Stephens, a Georgia politician and vice president of the Confederate States of America.

Stephens was welcomed home for the burial of the American flag. Many in his audience believed the Confederacy was destined to be an ocean-to-ocean slave empire—a realm that would stretch south from Virginia to Cuba, then take a sharp right turn west and slice off northern Mexico and southern California until it reached the Pacific.

Stephens rose to speak. He was a frail man with long bony fingers. His black suit and white shirt, topped with a large collar and billowing bow tie, made him look smaller than his 98 pounds. But the strength and intensity in his eyes left no doubt as to his dogged self-confidence.

Without notes he began. After several minutes, he paused, and then in a rush of words declared the cornerstone of the Confederate States of America rested "upon the great truth that the negro is not equal to the white man; that slavery subordination to the superior race is his natural and normal condition. This, our new government, is the first, in the history of the world, based upon this great physical, philosophical, and moral truth." The crowd inside and outside the hall broke into wild applause.

Seven hundred miles to the north in Philadelphia, however, an African American cabinetmaker, journalist, and lecturer crumpled the newspaper account of the Savannah speech. What Alexander Hamilton Stephens touted as a *great truth* was known by this man to be *the great lie*.

George E. Stephens—unrelated but with the same last name—was living proof that the idea of White racial superiority was no more than an excuse for enslaving four million African Americans in the South and for keeping a quarter-million free Blacks in the North from full liberty.

While the Stephens in Georgia dreamed of a slave empire, the Stephens in Philadelphia wanted to bury slavery and the greed that made enslavement seem normal. This Stephens worried that not enough African Americans in the North saw the coming of war as a chance to destroy American slavery and slaveholders.

George E. Stephens cried out:

˜AROUSE, FREE BLACK MEN! AROUSE! ACT—ACT IN THE LIVING PRESENT!˜

———————————◼––•◆•––◼———————————

The year before George E. Stephens's birth, a Black uprising changed his parents' life. The 1831 Nat Turner slave revolt and the bloodthirsty White retaliation that followed made eastern Virginia a dangerous place for free and literate African Americans of "mixed blood." George's parents, William and Mary, were free and literate. Both of their fathers were White slave owners and their mothers Black slaves. The young couple decided to move north after the Turner revolt, but first they needed approval from a committee of White citizens, and second, they had to promise never to return. With permission in hand and a fervent pledge made, William and Mary headed for Philadelphia where George was born in 1832.

In the City of Brotherly Love, however, George's parents discovered a frightening similarity between the slave-holding South and the free North. When George was two, Philadelphia experienced one of its periodic race riots. A street fight broke out when Blacks and Whites pushed and shoved one another to ride the city's newest entertainment sensation, the Flying Horses, a merry-go-round. White mobs beat and burned their way through the city's Black neighborhoods. By the time George was twelve, he had lived through five race riots.

George E. Stephens was described as a "promising young man" who possessed "a vigorous intellect and an easy flow of ideas." Although the city had no public high schools for African Americans, George's father, who worked shining shoes and waiting tables, found a school for his son—a free private high school for African Americans operated by Quakers. This religious group denounced slavery as evil, and their school stressed grammar, logic, and rhetoric as the basis for all learning.

The school also had a practical side—it taught students vocational trades. Stephens received a classical education for his mind and training as a cabinetmaker for his wallet. There are no records of how well he did, but at age twenty-one he became a founding member of the Banneker Institute, named for the Black mathematician Benjamin Banneker. This elite group of young, bright, and articulate African Americans met regularly to discuss self-improvement, rail against slavery, and debate the future of free people of color in the North.

Stephens found little work as a cabinetmaker. But with a wife, Susan, three stepchildren, and Susan's mother to support he needed steady work. The twenty-five-year-old took a job as supply clerk for the U.S. Coast Survey, a scientific organization. Aboard the USS *Walker* they sailed up and down the country's eastern seaboard surveying navigation routes.

In late November 1857, the *Walker* docked in Charleston, South Carolina, for a short stay. Stephens went ashore and observed one of the largest slave-trading centers in the world. With no sense that his light-brown skin color or wavy but African-textured hair might put him at risk, Stephens entered into the devil's den of slavery. He wrote to a friend, "You must witness it in all its loathsomeness."

A free African American almanac author and man of mathematics and science, Benjamin Banneker (1731–1806) served on the commission that surveyed the new Federal District (Washington, DC).

BENJAMIN BANNEKER
ASTRONOMER–CITY PLANNER

AT 22, USING A BORROWED WATCH AS A MODEL, A POCKET KNIFE AS HIS ONLY TOOL, HE CONSTRUCTED THE FIRST CLOCK MADE IN AMERICA.—IT KEPT ACCURATE TIME FOR OVER 20 YEARS!

ON THE ADVICE OF THOMAS JEFFERSON, HE WAS PLACED ON THE COMMISSION WHICH SURVEYED AND LAID OUT THE CITY OF WASHINGTON, D.C.!

PLANNING FOR PEACE IN TIME OF WAR WAS ADVOCATED BY BANNEKER IN HIS FAMOUS ALMANAC IN 1793!

Charleston's 42,000 residents included 19,000 slaves and 3,000 free people of color, plus 20,000 Whites. Everywhere Stephens wandered, he saw wealth built by slave labor, from the streets under his feet to the mansions on Broad Street.

South Carolina's lucrative rice and cotton crops were planted, grown, cultivated, and picked by slaves. Slave labor made rich slave owners. They required bankers to manage their wealth and lawyers to protect it. They needed slave dealers to sell them more slaves to make them richer. The making, managing, and protecting of this wealth turned Charleston into a jewel of a city, but underneath its shine lay thousands of enslaved workers.

Stephens witnessed a group of slaves being led off a ship, and it stunned him. Bound together with thick rope, the "half clad, filthy looking men women and children" were treated as farm animals—women with babies in their arms, young girls holding a crying child's hand, fathers with eyes weighed to the ground in helplessness, boys whose faces were marked by horror in realizing their parents could not protect them. After seeing people herded like livestock, people who could have been his relatives, Stephens described Charleston as a "half-way house on the pathway of wrong to the region of the damned."

Drifting through the city, Stephens seemed to be a trusted house servant or a Charleston free person of color. He attracted little attention. He was unaware, though, of the series of harsh Black Codes created to maintain White control, codes that outlawed him and any Black person from wearing fancy clothes, carrying a cane, beating a drum, singing in an African language, or smoking a cigar in public. Each crime was punishable by twenty lashes.

On December 15, his stay in that "half-way house" of a city took a nasty turn. Seen too many times coming and going from his ship, he was arrested—not for violating one of the Black Codes, but for being a Northern Black sailor.

To prevent African Americans from the North spreading anti-slavery discontent, South Carolina's Negro Seamen Act required all Black mariners to be jailed while their ship stayed in Charleston. Neither Stephens nor his captain knew of this law. The Seamen Act charged for the cost of jailing Black crew members. If a ship's captain did not pay, the crew was sold at the next slave auction.

A horrified Stephens waited in a dark, dank cell. His jailer refused to contact the *Walker*'s captain or allow him to write his wife. Stephens was in the hands of a jailer who only thought of him as a prime field hand worth as much as $1,000.

When his ship's lieutenant discovered what had happened and paid for his release, Stephens, a religious man, believed his prayers were answered. He hid aboard ship until the *Walker* left Charleston to return to Philadelphia. As the ship sailed out of Charleston's harbor in January, he stared at the smug waterfront mansions of rich slave owners and offered not a prayer, but a curse: "Death lays his icy hands on many a guilty head, and is the avenger of many a vile wrong—the finger of God is laid upon Charleston."

A year later, in 1859, Stephens met Robert Hamilton at a Banneker lecture in Philadelphia. Hamilton owned and co-published the *Anglo-African*, a weekly newspaper based in New York City for African Americans throughout the North. Hamilton liked what he heard Stephens say about Charleston and slavery, and asked him to write for his newspaper.

Stephens's first article appeared on November 14, 1859. He

George Stephens wrote for this popular four-page weekly newspaper published between 1859 and 1865.

17

argued against the popular colonization movement, an effort to encourage free African Americans to return to Africa. Many Whites, including Abraham Lincoln, and a few Blacks reasoned that African Americans could never be treated equally in the United States. They would be better off if they, like the Pilgrims, founded a colony in Africa. Stephens disagreed and asked, "Why should we feed the prejudices of the self-pampered Caucasian by indulging the hope that the despised negro will migrate to the sunlit shores of Africa?"

Two months later he called colonization the "mouth-piece of American prejudice and hatred." He warned readers to "[t]ake notice," because supporters of sending Blacks to Africa had one purpose: "[T]hat the negro shall remain in the country only in the condition of a slave."

At 4:30 on the morning of April 12, 1861, forty artillery guns slung shell after shell into the federal fortification, Fort Sumter, in Charleston's harbor. People in the city rushed to their rooftops and to the waterfront to witness and celebrate. Two and half days later, the eighty-four soldiers guarding Fort Sumter hoisted a white flag.

The Civil War had begun. News of the surrender raced across the country with headlines of "WAR!" Confederate president Jefferson Davis started raising an army of 100,000 men. Abraham Lincoln asked for 75,000 volunteers to put down the Confederate Rebellion.

Throughout the South and North, men rushed to volunteer for the excitement of war. African Americans in the North, however, ran smack into a 1792 federal law that restricted state militias to "free able-bodied white male[s]." And Pennsylvania governor Andrew Curtin went a step further. He threatened to arrest any militia officer who dared to march through Pennsylvania with even a single Black soldier. This dashed Stephens's dreams of a revenge march through the streets of Charleston.

Fort Sumter was hit with 1,800 shells from April 12–14, 1861, a siege that marked the beginning of the Civil War.

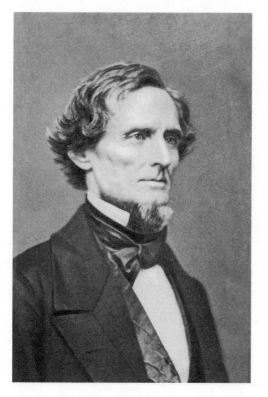

Jefferson Davis was president of the Confederate States of America. The former Mississippi senator was a West Point graduate and a veteran of the Mexican-American War (1846–1848), but his military advice often put him at odds with Confederate officers.

Race kept George E. Stephens out of the army and from his vow to return to Charleston as a soldier. But he wouldn't be stopped. He immediately found work as a personal servant and cook to an army officer—Captain Benjamin C. Tilghman of the Twenty-sixth Pennsylvania Regiment. The White captain hated slavery as much as Stephens. He supported Stephens's plan to write dispatches for the *Anglo-African* telling Black readers how both armies treated slaves.

On April 19, 1861, one week after the first cannonball plowed into Fort Sumter, Stephens led a mule loaded with two wicker baskets of the captain's dishes and silverware. He marched behind the Pennsylvania regiment toward Maryland. Federal law barred him from wearing a uniform or carrying a rifle. But Stephens carried something more lethal—pen and paper powered by his sharp mind.

CHAPTER TWO

WATCH NIGHT

For more than a year, Stephens and the Twenty-sixth Pennsylvania camped in southern Maryland between Baltimore and Washington, DC. Other regiments in the area shared the same duties: to prevent surprise attacks on Washington and to stop Maryland slaves from reaching freedom. Abraham Lincoln needed Maryland, a slave state, to remain in the Union. To make sure it did, the army had orders to return escaping slaves to their Maryland slaveholders.

As an army cook and servant, Stephens supported the first duty; but as an abolitionist, a person who opposed slavery, he disregarded the second. With his captain's quiet support, Stephens slipped onto tobacco plantations and directed slaves to the safest and swiftest path to Washington, where they could disappear into the community of 14,000 free African Americans.

Slaves who made it to other Union camps faced the fickle mercy of White soldiers—a few helped them escape, many returned them as ordered, some sold them and pocketed the money, while others abused them for sport or sex. Excepting the few who helped slaves escape, Stephens ranted about the rest in the *Anglo-African*: "the men of which this army is composed are drawn from the cesspools of society, and are intemperate, brutal and ignorant; pregnant with negro hate, and strangers to every sentiment of honor or justice."

In one story, he told how Frank, a Maryland slave, came into a Union camp pursued by a sheriff and "a posse of five persons." Because of army policy, the senior officer had no choice but to hand Frank over. The sheriff asked for an armed escort, which prompted Stephens's contempt: "[I]t required 13 men to take one boy of 15 years. Great Heavens, how many men would it require to re-enslave ten thousand full-grown men?"

Seventeen months of civil war had resulted in a near stalemate and cost the lives of 100,000 White men from the North. Abraham Lincoln needed another way to force the Confederates to end their rebellion. On September 22, 1862, he issued a threat. He announced a preliminary Emancipation Proclamation. As president and commander-in-chief of the army, Lincoln would proclaim freedom for slaves in the Confederacy—unless the Confederates ended their rebellion and returned to the United States. He gave a deadline of New Year's Day 1863, a hundred days away.

Lincoln's proclamation would slowly destroy the Confederacy's three-billion-dollar investment in slaves. It would also weaken the rebels' ability to fight should more slaves escape to freedom, knowing they would be free when they reached Union camps. Without slaves, Confederate soldiers would have to dig their own fortifications, grow and harvest food, and pick cotton to sell to Europe to buy weapons. The more soldiers working, the fewer fighting. Southern White soldiers digging trenches and picking cotton would leak energy from the rebel army.

In mid-November, with six weeks remaining until New Year's Day, the Union made a final attempt to persuade the Confederates to end the war. An army of 117,000 soldiers marched toward the

Confederate capital of Richmond, Virginia. And Stephens told *Anglo-African* readers that the Union Army was "in full advance on the Rebel Capital."

However, the advance stalled on the eastern bank of the Rappahannock River, halfway to Richmond. The Confederates had knocked out the bridge across the river and positioned 73,000 soldiers on the other side in the small town of Fredericksburg, Virginia. November weather kept daytime temperatures in the low twenties. Thick floes of ice warned that there'd be neither man nor beast nor gunpowder getting to the other side through the water. The Union Army had no choice but to wait for materials from Washington, fifty miles away, to build pontoon bridges— temporary bridges built on flotation barrels.

While they waited, Stephens kept busy tending to the captain's uniforms and meals, and helping Maryland slaves escape. In his November 20 *Anglo-African* dispatch, he reported the plight of George and Kitty Washington and four of their children, who in an icy rainstorm crept from the woods into his camp. Their owner had fled when the Union soldiers neared his plantation, and he'd taken

Abraham Lincoln's election caused eleven slave states to secede. When the Civil War followed, the inexperienced Lincoln faced the greatest crisis and threat to the United States of any president—human slavery, states' rights, and national unity.

The Battle at Fredericksburg, December 11, 1862, was another Union disaster early in the war. George Stephens, who observed the battle, was convinced Abraham Lincoln would have to issue the Emancipation Proclamation and allow African Americans into the Union Army.

the couple's two oldest children with him to Richmond. George and Kitty knew their owner would return for the rest of their family when the Union troops left. They faced a choice that, either way, would haunt them: remain enslaved with all of their six children, or run away so four could grow up free. The parents chose to sacrifice two to save four.

At first the family had joined seventy other plantation slaves heading for Washington, DC. George and Kitty carried the two youngest while two others walked, but the family's pace was too slow, and they could neither keep up nor stay ahead of the patrolling Confederate cavalry who had orders that "all negroes caught attempting to escape are . . . to be shot." The shivering family hid in the woods until Stephens welcomed, dried, and fed them before sending them on their fifty-mile walk to Washington.

Hunkered down along the Rappahannock River, Stephens and the Union Army waited a month before the needed materials arrived.

In laying the bridge, the unarmed engineers were easy prey for Confederate sharpshooters. When the bridge was completed, Union soldiers charged across and pursued the rebels out of Fredericksburg. The next morning they suffered. Trying to take the hills behind the town they charged into an open field. Well-placed cannon and rifle fire mowed down one advance after another. Hit by relentless firepower and unable to go forward, they retreated back across the river. The Union suffered 12,000 casualties; the Confederates lost 4,700.

Stephens watched the slaughter from the eastern side of the river. He described the carnage. "We could stand on the plains and see great heaps of dead."

White newspapers such as the *New-York Tribune* informed readers of the disaster, but Stephens gave his *Anglo-African* readers more: "[t]he great battle of Fredericksburg which has resulted in the total defeat of the Federal Army." And Stephens reported the cowardly behavior of the Twentieth New York Regiment, which had taken cover, along with their "colored servants," behind an embankment during the shelling, until "the officers and men drove [the servants] out at the point of the bayonet saying, 'Let the damned nigger be killed—how dare they come here among white men.' There, sir, in the very jaws of death, they did not forget to hate our brethren."

On frigid New Year's Eve 1862, Stephens sat inside his tent near Fredericksburg. After almost two years of fighting, four million African Americans remained enslaved. Holding a pencil in his numbed fingers, he wrote his final article of the year. Although it wouldn't appear for more than two weeks, he wanted readers to know his predictions. "If military necessity, three months ago, required emancipation, the military necessity of the present time must require it still the more." And he added, if emancipation was "withheld, it will be because slavery is preferred to honor, country, or right."

The last night of the year was also known as Watch Night, a time when Black churches in the North filled with people praying for a better year. On Watch Night 1862, they prayed for Abraham Lincoln and the Emancipation Proclamation, the freeing of slaves. But Stephens understood what the proclamation wouldn't do. By law Lincoln could only proclaim freedom for slaves held by the enemy—three-and-a-half million in eleven Confederate states—but *not* freedom for the half-million enslaved in Maryland, Delaware, Kentucky, and Missouri—the only slave states in the Union. Their rights to enslave continued to be protected by the Constitution. And the only way slaves held in the Confederacy could be free was by escaping or being liberated by the Union Army.

In spite of these limitations, Stephens wrote, "This December 31st, the watch-night of 1862, may be the watch-night which shall usher in the new era of freedom." He predicted it would "necessitate a general arming of the freedmen." Because fewer Whites were volunteering, Stephens believed Lincoln would have no choice but to call on African Americans to help liberate the slaves he declared free. But Stephens worried. After two years of being rejected by the army, would free African Americans in the North volunteer? Did they care enough to risk their lives to free other African Americans who were enslaved?

This *Harper's Weekly* cartoon shows the North's distress over the deaths of so many men in the Battle of Fredericksburg. Soaring Union casualties discouraged volunteers and led Abraham Lincoln to search for other ways to bring more men into the Union Army.

CHAPTER THREE

JAMES HENRY GOODING

Four hundred miles north of Stephens's flickering campfire, candles shimmered behind the frosted windows of New Bedford's Liberty Hall. On the first day of 1863, an arctic chill skittered off the Atlantic and emptied the streets of the Massachusetts whaling village. Inside Liberty Hall a young man "of medium height . . . brown skin, curly hair, and black eyes" sat on a hard bench in an anxious crowd. Henry Gooding had arrived at noon, eager for news, and squeezed in among the town's rich and poor, Black and White, women and men, whalers and bankers. All were listening to the speeches on the evils of slavery, singing, and waiting to hear whether Abraham Lincoln had signed the Emancipation Proclamation.

This day marked the expiration of Lincoln's warning to the Confederates. They were to end their rebellion or have their slaves declared free.

Hours passed. By eight o'clock, new spermaceti candles were lit, but no messenger had burst through the door. Gooding

Thousands of copies of the Emancipation Proclamation were printed and sold to the public. Many African American families hung a copy in their homes.

squirmed on the hard bench. No news yet from Washington—his thoughts bounced from one possible reason to another. Had White Northerners who didn't want their towns flooded with slave refugees pressured Lincoln not to issue the proclamation? Had Confederates, at the last minute, decided they needed their slaves more than independence and surrendered?

Gooding sang with less and less spirit through the hours, doubting the war would end and feeling his anxiety increase that slavery would continue.

Across town, at close to 11:00 p.m., the telegraph wires began to dance—word by slow word, each letter tapped in Washington and decoded in New Bedford, the words hand-copied and given to a messenger who raced to Liberty Hall. A boy threw open the heavy door and blew in on a gust of icy air. The Reverend William Jackson of Salem Baptist Church, president of the New Bedford Colored Association, read Lincoln's proclamation: "By virtue of the power in me vested as Commander-in-Chief . . . in time of actual armed rebellion against the authority and government of the United States . . . I do order and declare that all persons held as slaves . . . are, and henceforward shall be free."

Liberty Hall erupted. Cheers, hand-clapping, and loud voices. Hugs and handshakes followed.

Rev. Jackson continued. Near the end of his reading, Gooding shivered at the words—Lincoln's words: "And I further declare and make known, that such persons of suitable condition, will be received into the armed service of the United States."

Applause exploded again. After twenty months of turning African Americans away from the war effort, Abraham Lincoln called on Black men to help put down the rebellion and free Confederate slaves. With heavy strokes of his pen, Lincoln set aside his fear of arming African Americans and changed the Civil War from a fight to save the Union to a war to free slaves.

Whaling had made New Bedford one of the richest towns in America. For many years, New Bedford's whale oil had burned in the table lamps and streetlights throughout the Northeast. With whaling came jobs for any man willing to leave home for years to hunt whales. In the summer of 1856, whaling brought eighteen-year-old Henry Gooding to New Bedford. He quickly found work as a cook on the *Sunbeam* and left on a four-year whale hunt. He returned to New Bedford twice in search of more voyages. In six years, Gooding sailed in the Atlantic, Pacific, Indian, and Arctic Oceans, but in the summer of 1862, when the Civil War was well into its second year, he returned to New Bedford to stay.

That fall, he married Ellen Allan, a seamstress. Ellen's wavy hair was a gift from her mother, who was born in the Azores, a group of Atlantic islands off the coast of Portugal. Ellen's dark-brown coloring came from her father, who escaped slavery and settled in New Bedford. Fugitive slaves and Portuguese Africans from the Azores were two of the groups who came to New Bedford to work as whalers. The town's Quaker community made it one of the best places in America for the couple to settle. They were not restricted as to where they could live; Black men could vote and sit on juries; and their children could attend public schools—liberties denied in almost every other city and town in the North. In spite of New Bedford's advantages, Gooding craved to "forgo comfort, home, [and] fear" and join the war against slavery.

Gooding followed newspaper reports of the war, including George E. Stephens's stories of White soldiers' treatment of slaves. Later he would echo Stephens's writing, but with an underlined word for emphasis. "[W]hen the slave sees the white soldier approach, he dares not trust him and why? because he has heard that <u>some</u> have treated him worse than their owners in rebellion."

Gooding opposed slavery, not only because he was an African American and believed it morally wrong, but because he had been born a slave. On his seaman protection papers, which all whalers carried, he listed his parents as James and Sarah Gooding. The clerk issuing his papers described him as a "mulatto," or a person of mixed race. Gooding claimed he was born free in Troy, New York, but he'd been born a slave in Bern, North Carolina.

A White shopkeeper named James Gooding bought him from a slave owner when he was eight years old, took him to New York City, and left him in the Colored Orphan Asylum. Gooding never saw this man—his father—again. Afterward, he preferred to be called by his middle name, Henry, perhaps rejecting his namesake, a man who loved him enough to buy him out of slavery but who had abandoned him.

Gooding spent years in the orphanage cared for by Quaker women who gave him a rigorous classical education, not unlike the schooling Stephens had at his Quaker school in Philadelphia. But no amount of learning could hide the scars of Gooding's youth: hurt by a White father who did not love him enough to keep him, and a Black mother powerless to keep her eight-year-old son.

Gooding shared little about his life before coming to New Bedford. Historians speculate that he continued his education by reading and writing during the years he was at sea. In New Bedford, he arranged to have six of his poems printed for friends. His writing and passionate arguments against slavery led him to be elected vice president of the New Bedford Young Men's Anti-Slavery Society. James Bunker Congdon, a wealthy banker and founding member of New Bedford's Anti-Slavery Society, described Gooding as "a person of intelligence and cultivation." His letters and poetry showed a broad and deep knowledge of history, religion, and classical literature. One of his poems, written while at sea, evokes Gooding's longing for the mother he hardly knew:

> And when far away, I remember that Mother,
> Who, well do I know, was then weeping for me,
> Who tried, but in vain, her forebodings to smother,
> That danger was near her dear boy on the sea.

On January 21, 1863, the War Department authorized Mass-achusetts governor John Andrew to raise a regiment of "persons of African descent." It would be the state's fifty-fourth regiment. The first fifty-three had been White regiments, but the soldiers of the fifty-fourth would be Black, led by White officers. They would receive the same pay and uniforms as White regiments.

John Andrew had been elected governor at the time Abraham Lincoln became president. Radical Johnny, as Andrew's detractors called him, wanted an immediate end to slavery in every state. He believed the races were equal, both in the eyes of God and in the promise of the Declaration of Independence. And he wanted the Fifty-Fourth Massachusetts Infantry to "be a model for all future Colored Regiments." The governor also wanted Black officers for his regiment, but the War Department thought the idea too radical. No White soldier would salute or obey an order from a Black officer if their regiments were in the field together.

For his regiment, Governor Andrew needed a thousand Black men and twenty-eight White officers. Notices appeared all over Massachusetts—in New Bedford, Boston, Pittsfield, and any other town with a Black population:

COLORED MEN, ATTENTION!
YOUR COUNTRY CALLS!

On February 14, 1863, Gooding walked into the recruiting office on New Bedford's Williams Street and volunteered.

The publishers of the pro-Lincoln paper the *New Bedford Mercury* knew Gooding from his anti-slavery work. They asked him to write from the battlefield to tell readers what it was like to be part of a free African American regiment, fighting an enemy who believed in their enslavement. Gooding agreed to tell the story of the Fifty-Fourth in a series of weekly letters.

George E. Stephens was the first African American Civil War correspondent. Gooding became the second. Stephens's readers were Black, Gooding's mostly White. At times Gooding sounded

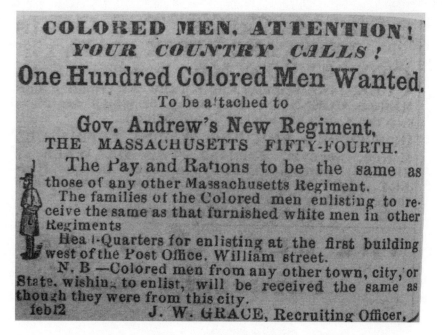

as if he needed to interpret African American thinking and feelings for his readers. And at times his tone hinted that he thought himself smarter than those he wrote about. In one of his first letters Gooding explained why Blacks in New Bedford were slow to volunteer: "They do not, some of them, yet exactly comprehend the future benefits of enlisting, but they have an impulse equally as great, so far as they are capable of understanding it, and that is revenge."

Not every African American in New Bedford shared Gooding's eagerness for the army, and that caused him to criticize those who did not. In his first published letter he asked: "Are the colored men here in New Bedford, who have the advantage of education, so blind to their own interest[?]"

For those Black men, the risk of being killed ran deep, but distrust and fear of being mistreated by the War Department ran deeper. Of New Bedford's 115 Black men of army age, only 34 volunteered. New Bedford missed its 100-man goal.

The small company chose Gooding and twenty-three-year-old William Carney as two of their sergeants. Carney, an escaped slave from Norfolk, Virginia, arrived in New Bedford as a fifteen-year-old.

On March 4, Henry and Ellen Gooding walked from their rooms on South Water Street to New Bedford's City Hall and waited as other volunteers and families gathered. They made their way to the train station, and Gooding wrote later that he marched "for honor, duty and liberty." That afternoon, the thirty-four New Bedford men marched from a train station a few miles south of Boston into Camp Meigs. They were accompanied by a drummer boy's drumbeat and the shrill sounds of a fife player. The few soldiers already at the desolate camp cheered as they arrived.

Gooding walked on wooden planks laid over muddy snow and squished his way to a barrack large enough to sleep a hundred. His first minutes of army life began with a series of rapid orders that had him "examined, sworn in, washed & uniformed," and left him speechless as the clothes carefully chosen by Ellen were carried outside and burned.

Dressed in his Union Blues—light blue pants and a dark blue jacket with eight brass eagle buttons—Gooding wasted no time in telling *New Bedford Mercury* readers they were "looking quite like soldiers." And that "Col. Shaw is on the ground, doing all he can do for the comfort of those now in camp."

Colonel Robert Gould Shaw, a twenty-five-year-old White officer with a baby face and chilly blue eyes, had arrived at camp the day before Gooding. Governor Andrew wanted a White officer free of color prejudice; Shaw fell short of that goal. He was not an abolitionist. He believed the Emancipation Proclamation had turned the Civil War into a "war of extermination." He was, however, an army officer determined that the Fifty-Fourth would be as good as any. At first Shaw described himself as a "Nigger Col." But after weeks of drilling he admitted, "The intelligence of the men is a great surprise to me."

clerical and lay representa-
al Churches in this vicinity,
nual meeting on Tuesday at
rch, Fairhaven, at 11 o'clock

s organized by the choice of
ion, moderator. After intro-
moderator and the reading of
he previous meeting by the
ssion was devoted to exercises
nce.

the Conference re-assembled.
part for devotional exercises,
audience was entertained by
s of the varied experience of
since the last meeting of the
nainder of the afternoon was
ng topic, "The best arrange-
ervices of the Sabbath." The
pated in by many, both minis-
rs, and the prevalent opinion
ecided in favor of the good old
, two sermons a day, sabbath
llowed by a meeting for prayer
evening.

was devoted to the discussion
cal importance to the churches.
of doctrinal truth to exper-
emarks on this topic set forth
e forms the fact, that God's
on is by the truth, and con-
hest style of preaching is that
nderstanding, rather than that
ne emotional nature. Second,
pew on the pulpit."

s.—The Old Colony Conference
l its meetings Wednesday fore-
gational church, Fairhaven.
morning session, commencing
, was devoted to a season of
was conducted by Rev. Mr.
, and though not numerously
interesting to those who were
scripture, which gave principal
hts of the speakers during the
ount recorded in the Gospel of
Jesus in the ship in the midst

pent in transacting the usual
ence.
11 o'clock a congregation as-
ervices, but in the absence of
who was detained by illness.
Bedford, delivered an excel-
he words of our Savior, Matt.
, not as I will, but as thou
with those other words of the
"Even so Father; for so it
ght."
r was impressively celebrated,
Middleboro', and Rev. James

Letter from the 54th (Colored) Regiment.

MORRIS ISLAND, Oct. 10, 1863.

MESSRS. EDITORS:—The monotony of life was some-
what broken last Monday night, October 5th, by an
insane attempt by the rebels to either capture or destroy the Ironsides. Their plans to destroy the vessel, were, to place torpedoes under her, and blow her
up. The attacking party came down out of the inner
harbor about 9 o'clock, passed the two monitors lying
between Gregg and Moultrie, hugging themselves in
the belief that they were unseen. But the ever watch-
ful tars were very well aware of all the rebel man-
œuvres. They let them go ahead, as it was the intention of the navy to trap the bold rascals. After
the rebels had made the distance opposite the Ironsides, by running close along the beach of Sullivan's
Island, they struck boldly, but cautiously out for their
prize. On they came, with muffled oars; but while
they were approaching, the crew of the Ironsides were
silently preparing to give their nocturnal or (infernal)
visitors a warm reception. At length the rebel boats
are within hailing distance—the marine on the bow
of the Ironsides, cries—"boat ahoy!" no response
from the boats, but sudden and vigorous strokes with
the oars, and shouts of, "pull hard! the Yankees
are all turned in—we've got her sure—pull, pull, lets
get aboard before they awake." A rocket from the
Ironsides told the monitors to begin—out of their
huge guns, they threw grape, cannister and shrapnel—
the crew of the 'old invincible' mounted the railing,
and poured down a continual stream of minnie balls,
which must have convinced the unlucky rebels that the
Yankees were wide awake. Another nice little Yankee invention was used to advantage on this occasion;
it is almost as nice as 'Greek Fire;' it is a contrivance
to squirt steam. One party of rebels who were to place
the torpedoes under the vessel, got out of range,
and pulled round to that side of the ships not in action, and got so close as to warrant them in throwing
their infernals into the water, when lo! the skin-peel-
ing element was in their midst! It is needless to say
that they dropped their infernal machines, and inten-
tions too. They could not stand such a novel mode of
warfare as that, so they pulled for the nearest land
under the control of Beaury—Sullivan's Island. I
believe we did not take many prisoners, as the rebels
decamped sooner than the officers supposed they
would. We are waiting to hear another protest, or
bull, by little "Peter," against squirting steam.

While the navy was doing such active service, the
land forces were all prepared and waiting for an inva-
sion of this right little, tight little isle. There was
no surety, but the rebels, by attracting all our attention to one point, would come like an avalanche on
some other, as they agree that this island is their
greatest loss. But they troubled us no more that
night, nor will they be apt to for some time.

The attempt of the rebels to get possession of or
destroy the Ironsides is pretty conclusive evidence that
they admire her qualities as a fighting ram, or have a
wholesome dread of her capacity to prove their ob-
structions all bosh. We shall no doubt be posted on
her abilities that way soon, as matters appear to be
coming to a point. Couriers ride, as if for dear life,
bearing ponderous and ominous looking envelopes;

The following is a sum
by steamers Hibernia and
The total stock of cott
including 41,000 bales, i
The Bank of France h
count to 5 per cent, ow
specie. The political nev
tant character.
The ship Hahneman, o
been fired into and board
the first of July. After e
Hahneman, the private
lon. 35 west.
The Daily News says,
received by the Adriatic,
Chattanooga, that is do
hopes of our pro-souther
convinces us of overratin
friends.
The Paris corresponde
as follows:—In referenc
Stephens, the Vice Pre
States, is coming to Pari
the French government,
relative to the abolition o
little more comfort for M
It says it knows nothing
all events the abolition o
pensible condition of any
European people and go
encouraging for the sout
and not only slavery but
the very thing they have
It is stated that the Pr
will probably be marrie
(to whom she has been
the ensuing spring.
The King of the Greek
The health of Lord Ly
apprehension; but the la
vorable. His great age
against his recovery.
W. S. Lindsay, Membe
at considerable length up
agricultural dinner. In
he denied the assertion of
jority of the people of Eu
States. The noble Earl
spoken the sentiment of
If the North had gone
putting an end to slave
his colleagues would hav
a very large majority of
flict was entered into, a
with no such end in view
ceedings which had beer
enlistment act, he said h
the land respected, but
not see why they should
from being supplied with
continued to be supplied
of the war he had no dou
separation and not reunic
had elapsed he believed
cut up, not merely into
States
The Mexican deputat
Mexico to the Arch Duke
by the Grand Duke on th
gives the following as h
the Mexican assembly o
deeply. It cannot but
our House, that they h
giance to the descendant
though the mission of ma
and welfare of Mexico

This abolitionist newspaper published Gooding's weekly letters, which gave hometown readers news of the Fifty-Fourth.

The "comfort" Gooding wrote about started at 5:30 a.m. with the regiment shivering to attention outside the barracks for a "count," then quickly hauling their bedding out to air, eating a hearty breakfast, and slogging through a full day of marching and drilling in one of the empty, barn-like barracks. Gooding learned to carry thirty pounds of equipment on his back and to march left, right, and forward with precision. He mastered the sharp 180-degree about-faces as smoothly as if on ice skates. He no longer had to think about how to change directions in perfect sync with the entire company, which had grown to a hundred soldiers. Two months into training, Gooding's legs were strong, his back soldier-straight, and his pride in the Fifty-Fourth high.

Each day, after marching, drilling, and pulling additional guard or work duty, he would return to the barracks exhausted and work on his weekly *Mercury* letter. Gooding shared only good news—"The glorious 54th . . . is getting on nicely." He wanted to encourage others to join him and the Fifty-Fourth Massachusetts Infantry.

Every soldier knew the risk of war. But for African Americans there was a greater risk. Jefferson Davis, the Confederate president, issued his own proclamation, published in papers throughout the North: "negroes found with arms to be immediately hung."

Gooding accepted the Confederate threat and wrote from camp: "There is not a man in the regiment who does not appreciate the difficulties, the dangers, and maybe ignoble death that awaits him, if captured by the foe, and they will die upon the field rather than be hanged like a dog."

CHAPTER FOUR

CALL TO COURAGE

The Union Army needed Black soldiers, and Philadelphia had the largest African American population in America. Governor Curtin, however, refused to raise a Pennsylvania regiment. In the spring of 1863, Massachusetts was the only state accepting Black men.

Governor Andrew had to hire recruiters to search for volunteers outside of Massachusetts because there weren't enough African Americans in the state to fill a 1,000-man regiment. He reached out as far north as Canada, west to Missouri, and south to Pennsylvania.

Stephens was hired as a recruiter for Philadelphia. He recruited at churches, civic organizations, and large recruiting rallies. His *Anglo-African* battlefield stories and his reputation from the Banneker Institute made him a popular speaker. He challenged his audiences' manly and racial pride by preaching they were as brave as White men. They must prove their courage. They must defend the country and their race by volunteering for the Fifty-Fourth.

Stephens also challenged in print. He wrote that if Black volunteers failed to join, "[w]e would be ranked with the most depraved and cowardly of men." But no matter how hoarse his voice became or how ink-stained his fingers, many remained skeptical. To the doubters, the army wanted them now because it was losing the war and fewer Whites were volunteering.

White resistance convinced some African Americans it was futile to think they would be treated better for defending the country. Many Whites believed African Americans wouldn't fight or weren't disciplined enough to be soldiers. Some feared that, once armed, Black soldiers would seek revenge for 250 years of enslavement. Still other Whites would not accept the idea of Blacks fighting Whites, even White enemies. A group of White Philadelphians protesting the Emancipation Proclamation and African American soldiers issued a statement: "[A]ll attempts, directly and indirectly, on the part of the Federal Government to frustrate this intention, or change the relative status of the superior white, and inferior black races . . . are subversive of the original design [of the Constitution]."

The growing number of casualties, however, began to chip away at White attitudes. In 1862 a New York corporal, in a letter to his sister, wrote, "We don't want to fight side and side with the nigger. . . . We think we are . . . too superior [a] race." But a year later, in a show of twisted logic and misspellings, a battlefield-hardened soldier wrote his mother, "i would a little rather see a nigers head blowed of then a white mans."

The need for more soldiers continued to grow, yet Northern states refused to fund Black regiments. (But they counted African Americans who joined the Fifty-Fourth Massachusetts as part of their quotas they sent to the Union Army.)

To enlist more Black soldiers the federal government

created the Bureau of United States Colored Troops, or USCT. Massachusetts and Connecticut were the only states whose regiments kept their state identification. An Ohio regiment, for example, became the Fifth USCT, but the Fifty-Fourth remained a Massachusetts regiment, reporting through the governor to the War Department.

<hr />

In spite of doubts about the Union Army, more Black men volunteered for the war against slavery. Stephens and other recruiters had been successful. Gooding reported on the growing numbers. At the end of March 1863, there were 368 in camp; in April, 674; and by May, the regiment was full, with enough men to start another regiment, the Fifty-Fifth Massachusetts Infantry.

Stephens, pleased with his success in recruiting more than 200 men, decided it was time to do what he'd wanted to since the first day of the war: become a soldier. He left for Massachusetts. To reach Camp Meigs he traveled like a wanted criminal. In Philadelphia, young White men who despised the idea of Black soldiers searched the train station for anyone suspected of going to Boston. A White abolitionist bought Stephens's ticket for him, and when changing trains in New York City, he stayed in the shadows. Fernando Wood, the mayor of New York City at the war's onset, wanted the city to secede rather than lose money from the lucrative Southern cotton trade, which shipped through the city. The mayor assured the city council that secession would have "the whole and united support of the Southern States." Irish immigrants in New York, who competed with African Americans for jobs, feared the city would be flooded with slave refugees. New York City had become a dangerous place for African Americans during the Civil War.

On Thursday, April 30, 1863, the thirty-two-year-old Stephens walked into Camp Meigs and became one of the oldest to join the Fifty-Fourth. After two years *with* the army as a civilian cook and servant, and three months as a paid recruiter, Stephens was now *in* the army.

And with the eye of a veteran, he told readers, "I do not exaggerate when I say that there is no regiment superior, if equal to this in physique and aptitude of its men."

What Stephens didn't know but would soon find out was that Colonel Shaw subjected his soldiers to severe and uncompromising discipline. Shaw drilled the men to exhaustion. He marched them morning and afternoon in empty barracks with pounds of equipment on their backs, and when the ground dried out, he marched them outside under an unforgiving eye. He ordered them to bed at 8:00 p.m. and expected them to be asleep by 8:30, ready to start again the next morning. Bad behavior or slacking off met tough punishment. For serious infractions he had a gag stuffed into

Bucking and gagging was a form of punishment used in the Civil War in both Black and White regiments. This image shows a soldier before he is gagged. A log is placed under his knees and over his elbows. His hands and ankles are tied together.

Marching under guard while wearing a sign proclaiming the rule broken was one of the milder forms of punishment used in the Civil War.

the offender's mouth, a log placed under the knees and over the elbows, and the offender's hands and ankles tied together, making it impossible to move. Being hog-tied and fearing suffocation for as long as twelve hours reduced a man to a crying baby in soiled pants. When released, the sobbing soldier struggled to walk or even crawl.

For minor infractions, the soldiers were forced to stand on a barrel for hours with a sign citing the rule they had broken, or after a day's long march, they were ordered to continue marching in a circle with rocks added to their knapsacks. For some, the training, discipline, and possibility of dying led them to desert. When that happened, Shaw sent his officers into nearby towns to find the deserters and march them at gunpoint back to camp, where they were tied, gagged, and made to suffer.

The day Stephens reached camp, a shipment of Enfield rifles arrived. Both the Union and Confederate Armies used the rifle, designed and manufactured in Enfield, England. It fired a Minié or "minnie" ball—a half-ounce conical bullet of soft lead with exterior grooves for spiraling, or "rifling," out of the barrel. On contact, the spinning bullet shredded flesh, shattered bones, and left a huge and ragged exit wound that few would survive. In the hands of a sharpshooter, the Enfield was accurate up to 600 yards, or the length of six modern-day football fields. And in close combat, it could be fitted with a fifteen-inch bayonet.

Gooding announced the rifles' arrival and boasted to his readers back home, "[T]hey intend us to make good use of them; and I doubt not if the opportunity presents itself, they will be made good use of." But he did not share the challenge or the days and days of practice needed to master the front-loading rifle-musket with battlefield speed. In rapid order he had to:

> fish from his cartridge box a paper packet filled with gunpowder and bullet,
>
> rip it open with his teeth,
>
> pour the gunpowder neatly into the barrel, followed by the bullet,
>
> remove the ramrod attached to the rifle,
>
> insert the rod into the muzzle and ram the bullet down tight against the powder,
>
> reattach the ramrod,
>
> half-cock the hammer,
>
> grab a firing cap from a belt pouch and force it into the

firing cone,
fully cock the hammer,
aim with a steady hand, and
fire without jumping as the man next to him did the same.

He also had to learn not to be startled by the rifle's kick or the smoke floating into his eyes and nose. Then he had to do it all again: tear open the packet, pour the black powder down the barrel without spilling, ram a bullet tight with the ramrod (using just one finger, to avoid losing a whole hand if the gun accidentally fired), half-cock the hammer, insert the firing cap, fully cock the hammer, and fire, all the while shutting out noise and stinging smoke. Then repeat, as fast as he could, as many times as demanded, until he could load and fire three times a minute.

And this was only practice—hard enough with a barking officer in your face and a sergeant cursing in your ears. In battle, there'd be added smoke and fury, but also bullet balls of Confederate lead spinning toward him. His life depended on how fast he could load, fire, and reload.

Colonel Shaw reduced all acting sergeants to privates. He would decide who would make the best leaders and choose a sergeant for each of the ten companies of 100 soldiers, A to K. (For unknown reasons there was no J Company.) Shaw chose Stephens for B Company, and William Carney, but not Gooding, for C Company.

Gooding was intelligent, articulate, and popular, but Shaw did not think him the right man to lead soldiers into battle. On May 10, 1863, Stephens, Carney, and eight others sewed sergeant's stripes onto their blue uniform jackets, to show their rank and responsibility. There were no stripes for Private Gooding to sew. Stephens and Carney would receive $17 a month and Private Gooding, $13.

During his three months in camp, Gooding realized he preferred writing for the *Mercury* and underlining words for emphasis rather than keeping track of whether he had loaded powder into the barrel before the bullet, and whether he had packed it hard enough to fire. Writing was more comfortable than clicking a bayonet to his rifle and jabbing at make-believe cavalrymen, knowing that someday they would be real. Gooding's grand ideas of glory ran face-first into the reality that war was where you went to kill or be killed. Nevertheless he held to his belief that he and the Fifty-Fourth would "vindicate a foul aspersion that they were not men."

CHAPTER FIVE

HOPE AND GLORY

The Fifty-Fourth's special train chugged into Boston on Thursday morning, May 28, 1863. Before the engine came to a complete stop, Sergeant Stephens threw open the doors of one car and Private Gooding stepped from another. People on the platform gasped. One thousand Black soldiers in blue uniforms, with rifles on their shoulders and bayonets swinging from their hips, stepped through clouds of hissing steam.

Outside the station, Colonel Shaw, who had spent the night in Boston, waited on his horse. Spectators stared, unsure of what to say or how to react to something they had never witnessed before. Ten companies of a hundred men each, led by White officers and Black sergeants, marched with precision out of the station and fell into formation under Shaw's icy gaze.

Stephens scanned the crowd for any sudden or unusual movement—the colonel had warned that a mob might attack as they paraded to the State House for the governor's review. Shaw had armed each soldier with six cartridges and Minié balls and ordered the last company, the rear guard, to fix bayonets.

The *Boston Pilot*, a Catholic newspaper, had for months ridiculed the idea of Black soldiers and agitated its Irish readers: "One Southern regiment of white men would put twenty regiments of them to flight in half an hour. Twenty thousand negroes on the march would be smelled ten miles distant. No scouts need ever to be sent out to discover such warriors."

With a mob threat on his mind and an undecided crowd watching every move, Shaw circled the regiment for a final inspection. Satisfied, he took his place behind the color guard, where one soldier carried the American flag and one the Massachusetts state flag, both flanked by tall, muscular soldiers with rifles. In front of the color guard wiggled a drum corps of eight- to ten-year-old Black boys and a band of older White musicians.

With a nod from the colonel, the drum corps tapped out a beat, the band readied their instruments, and a squad of a hundred policemen with nightsticks in hand formed a line on both sides of the regiment. Colonel Kurtz, Boston's Chief of Police and a retired army officer, had made sure of no mob interference. Along the parade route, another hundred or more plainclothes policemen, with concealed hickory sticks, mingled among the 20,000 spectators.

Confident that six thousand Minié balls and a hundred bayonets could put down any riot, the Fifty-Fourth marched with such a trained grace that a reporter for the *Boston Commonwealth* asked, "Can we believe our own eyes and ears? Is this Boston? Is it America?"

Stephens marched with his yellow sergeant's stripes showing boldly on his sleeves, proud to be on his way to avenge the suffering inflicted on his parents, half of his grandparents, and as far back as his family stories of slavery and freedom carried him.

With an Enfield rifle heavy on his shoulder, Stephens marched along the parade route over streets bloodied for liberty in 1770, when British soldiers shot and killed five colonists, including a fugitive from slavery named Crispus Attucks. And Stephens marched down streets bloodied in 1851 in a fight to save Thomas Sims, and again in 1854 in a skirmish to save Anthony Burns—both fugitives forcibly taken back into bondage. Governor Andrew had arranged the parade route to honor Boston's history in the fight for liberty, but Stephens marched for the future, and for revenge. "The fangs of the serpent of oppression [have] pierced my own bosom, until it swells with the hot blood of a revenge which nothing but the blood of a slaveholder can satiate."

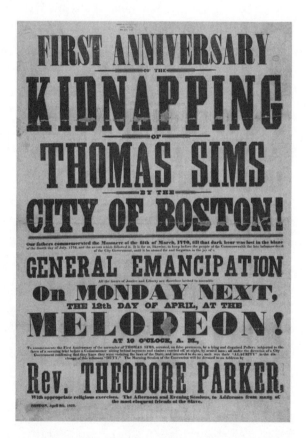

Sims, a fugitive, was arrested and returned to slavery under heavy police and army guard in April 1851. Sims escaped again and returned to Boston. He was one of the 20,000 who cheered the Fifty-Fourth as they marched to the Boston wharf to sail to South Carolina.

Gooding marched five rows behind Stephens. As the regiment neared a building at the corner of Beacon and Somerset Streets, he saw men at a window lower the shade, raise it, and lower it again. Many of the members of the Somerset Club, a social club for Boston's wealthy, owned textile mills that depended on southern cotton to make cloth. They wanted the Union to settle for peace and let the Confederacy go its own way. A few club members, however, stood on the steps applauding.

Gooding marched with a mix of emotions: happy for what he was doing, sad that his wife Ellen couldn't afford to travel from New Bedford to see him in his proudest moment. He had sent her his $50 state bounty the regiment received the week before, but there was no word when the army would start their monthly pay. In his last letter from Camp Meigs, however, Gooding wrote with button-busting pride: "The citizens of this Commonwealth need not be ashamed of the 54th now; and if the regiment will be allowed a chance, I feel confident the Colored Volunteers will add glory to her already bright name."

--- * * * ---

The regiment halted in front of the Massachusetts State House. There Governor Andrew stood watching with his special guests, including Frederick Douglass, a former slave who became the world's most famous abolitionist. Douglass had recruited his sons, Lewis and Charles, to the Fifty-Fourth. The mayor of Boston joined the governor and Douglass to march with the regiment down Beacon Street and through the Charles Gate of the Boston Common, a public park where, two centuries earlier, cows were pastured and criminals hanged.

More than five thousand admirers stood on the grassy lawn waiting for Colonel Shaw to snap a command. And when it came, ten company sergeants shouted out orders, sending a thousand soldiers into a dizzying whirl of elaborate battle drills and maneuvers needed to attack, defend, and, if necessary, retreat.

Stephens and the other nine sergeants guided their companies through the manual of arms, a series of precise movements with the rifle. Onlookers admired the synchronized dance of a thousand rifles twirling in rapid motion, smacking against shoulders, and stamping the ground in a stunning ballet, as if the ten-pound rifles were feather-light batons.

A reporter agreed: "No white regiment from Massachusetts has surpassed the Fifty-fourth in excellence of drill, while in general discipline, dignity, and military bearing the regiment is acknowledged by every candid mind to be all that can be desired."

At noon the Fifty-Fourth marched out of the Boston Common. Along the way, the men sang "John Brown's Body," a spirited marching song in honor of the abolitionist executed four years

John Brown (1800–1859) was a radical abolitionist who attempted to lead a slave revolt in what is now West Virginia.

earlier for leading a raid of Black and White men on a federal arsenal at Harper's Ferry, Virginia (now West Virginia). Brown had tried but failed to spark a slave revolt because only a few slaves joined him.

On the morning of his execution, Brown left an ominous note: "I John Brown am now quite <u>certain</u> that the crimes of this <u>guilty land: will</u> never be purged <u>away</u>; but with Blood."

The Fifty-Fourth would sail to South Carolina and become a regiment in the Union's Department of the South. Stephens and Gooding were on their way to the war John Brown had prophesied, and they joined the others in singing:

John Brown's body lies a-mouldering in the grave,
John Brown's body lies a-mouldering in the grave,
John Brown's body lies a-mouldering in the grave,
But his soul goes marching on.

Glory, Glory, Hallelujah!
Glory, Glory, Hallelujah!
Glory, Glory, Hallelujah!
His soul goes marching on.

John Brown's note warning of a war over slavery.

CHAPTER SIX

I SHALL BURN THIS TOWN

Wednesday, June 10, 1863: Out of Boston, the Fifty-Fourth now camped on an abandoned plantation on the Georgia coast.

Henry Gooding sat outside his tent. For readers of the *Mercury*, he'd begun his first letter from the South. But he stopped writing to watch a steamboat docking at the plantation wharf. Colonel Shaw rushed to meet it. On board, an officer with a bushy beard and dark eyes surveyed the camp. Without saying good morning or stepping off his boat, Colonel James Montgomery challenged the much younger Shaw: "How soon can you be ready to start on an expedition?"

"In half an hour," came Shaw's winded reply. Then came the drummer boy's signal for companies to fall into formation. Word raced from soldier to soldier, from tent to tent. *Our first action.* Soldiers grabbed rifles and checked cartridge boxes. Gooding put away his pencil and paper, picked up his rifle, and joined C Company.

Twenty-five-year-old Colonel Robert Gould Shaw was a two-year veteran of the Civil War when he assumed command of the Fifty-Fourth.

George Stephens marched B Company down the barren slope to the docks, followed by the other companies. Colonel Montgomery, the senior commander, took his measure of each company as they approached.

Decision made: C and F companies would stay behind for guard duty. The rest of the Fifty-Fourth steamed farther upriver for its first battle.

There would be no fighting yet for Gooding. He spent the night in a near-empty camp, concerned more about snakes than sneaking rebel soldiers. By sunrise the regiment had failed to return. By late morning, Gooding had reason to worry—faint sounds of artillery could be heard. And in the afternoon, clouds of smoke and the bitter smell of burning wood drifted down the river.

Colonel James Montgomery served as commander of a brigade made up of two Black regiments: his own Second South Carolina and Shaw's Massachusetts Fifty-Fourth.

Throughout the second night and into the next day, Gooding grew more and more anxious. What had happened?

While Gooding paced and worried about the regiment, Stephens settled comfortably on Montgomery's ship. The steamer moved up the Altamaha River where it was joined by three other Navy ships: a transport ship of Montgomery's soldiers and two gunboats with smooth-bore cannons for blasting coastal forts.

Eight companies of the Fifty-Fourth volunteers and five from Montgomery's Black regiment the Second South Carolina, consisting of former slaves, packed the ships with 1,300 soldiers. They were heading to the town of Darien, Georgia.

Within an hour, however, the invading armada ran aground in low tide and spent the night waiting for the morning's tidal change. They steamed on. From a ridge overlooking the river, the Confederate Twentieth Georgia Cavalry followed their movement. Montgomery taunted them by shelling houses on both banks of the river. He showed no concern over whether civilians or soldiers were inside.

Ahead of the arriving Union Army, Darien residents had fled.

Darien, one of Georgia's oldest and wealthiest towns, had ninety or so houses for its 500 White residents, in contrast to the hundreds of crude shanties housing 1,500 Black slaves on nearby plantations. Crowded along the riverbank, a lumber mill and warehouses bulged with rice, cotton, and timber to be shipped to Europe. This was the source of the town's wealth.

Blue-coated Black soldiers marched up from the river into the public square. In the center of town was a broad street flanked by mulberry and oak trees dripping with Spanish moss. Around the square stood the courthouse, a school, and three churches. In the shadows of this postcard picture were the means of controlling Darien's slaves—the jail and whipping post.

For the men of the Second South Carolina, the town was very much like ones where they and their families had been enslaved for generations, chopping, sawing, harvesting, and hauling to make someone else rich. For Stephens, who had almost been sold into slavery, the quiet, clean beauty of Darien hid the brutality that made it possible.

Except for a couple of elderly White women who refused to leave their homes and a handful of slaves whose owners hadn't thought them worth the trouble of moving, the town was empty, undefended, and at the mercy of the hundreds of soldiers who carried memories of places like Darien.

Montgomery ordered the town looted and his soldiers broke ranks and ran toward the houses. Forced to obey his senior officer, Shaw pointed to his right and ordered one of his officers to "take twenty men from the right of your company, break into the houses on this street, take out anything that can be made useful in camp."

Stephens and the rest of the regiment stood in place as soldiers went from house to house picking items that would turn sparse tents into luxury camps. When the plundering ended, Montgomery leaned in and told Shaw with a smile and in a low voice,

"I SHALL BURN THIS TOWN."

Shaw shook his head.

Montgomery whispered, "We are outlawed, and therefore not bound by the rules of regular warfare." He ordered his soldiers and one company of the Fifty-Fourth to douse the houses in turpentine and set them on fire. Some South Carolina soldiers also burned the whipping post, and Stephens's men ripped down the Confederate flag from the courthouse.

With the town in flames, the soldiers headed back to the river. Before boarding, they set fire to the cotton and lumber warehouses, which sent sheets of flames out toward the river. The four ships moved a safe distance from the flames, but it was too dark to travel down the winding waterway. They anchored for the night and then sailed back to camp the next morning.

Gooding saw how wrong he'd been to worry. Late on the third day after the companies had left, soldiers stepped off the ships laughing and singing as if returning from a church picnic. They lugged sofas, bed frames, tables, pianos, paintings, books, rugs, and more. They brought live chickens and pigs, and one soldier pulled a cow at the end of a rope made from ripped-up bedsheets.

Stephens, pleased with their raid, called Colonel Montgomery "[o]ur active and brave leader." He boasted, "When we left at sundown the whole town was enveloped in flames." He said they "steamed gaily down river" and "greeted the outbuildings with sundry iron missiles." Stephens ended his report, "The first rebel flag captured was captured by the 54th . . . by my company."

Southern newspapers called the raid the work of "nigger guerillas" and "cowardly Yankee negro thieves." Outrage was not limited to the South. Shaw's future brother-in-law wrote, "[I]nstead of improving the negro character and educating him for a civilized independence, we are re-developing all his savage instincts."

Gooding agreed with Stephens but saw no reason to explain that he had remained in camp. "After our forces landed, there was not more than 20 inhabitants to be seen in the place, the most of those were slaves and women; so there was no chance to show what sort of fighting material the Fifty-fourth is made of. . . . The town of Darien is now no more; the flames could be distinctly seen from the camp on the Island from three o'clock in the afternoon till daylight the next morning."

Fewer than three weeks after Darien, Stephens's opinion of Montgomery changed. Early on Saturday morning, June 27, while on guard duty, Stephens arrested a deserter from Montgomery's regiment. He marched the quivering soldier back to the Fifty-Fourth and South Carolina camp.

The deserter had been freed from slavery in one of Montgomery's bushwhacking raids and forced into the Union Army. The *freeman* quickly learned he had no say in what he could do or where he could go, and he had yet to be paid for his work. The difference between being a Northern soldier and a Southern slave was that, as a soldier, he had a better chance of being killed. That difference, Stephens believed, led former slaves to desert.

Stephens turned his prisoner over to Montgomery, who asked the deserter with the sweetness of a Sister of Mercy, "Is there any reason why you should not be shot?"

The stunned deserter, trying to please, mumbled "No, Sir."

"Then, be ready to die at 9:30."

Within an hour, the deserter was led to the edge of a field as a small band of musicians played a "dead march." Both regiments formed in a large U-shape, with the prisoner standing at the top. Guards placed a blindfold over the deserter's eyes and pinned a target over his heart so his face wouldn't be shot away. The chaplain, on his knees, prayed for the man's soul. There were no flags to flutter in the sea breeze, just 2,000 grim-faced soldiers standing at attention, trying to block out the muffled crying from the deserter. The chaplain finished his prayer, rose, and quickly moved to a safe distance.

A firing squad took position ten paces in front of the prisoner and upon the command of "Ready!" brought their rifles up.

At the shout of "Fire!" eight Minié balls lifted the prisoner off his feet, and he was dead before blood could stain his blue Union jacket.

Each man filed past the corpse, a reminder of what happened to deserters. Stephens had seen dead soldiers at Fredericksburg, but this was different. He had played a role in the man's death. He had stood only a few yards away, heard bullets hit flesh, and saw his prisoner, a former slave only a few weeks into freedom, fall dead in a cotton field like the one where he'd spent his whole life.

Gooding chose not to write about the deserter or the execution. He would do nothing to discourage other African Americans from volunteering. Stephens delayed writing about it for nine months. And even then he said little, except, "I am the man who brought him to justice or injustice." To write more he would have had to describe a murder by an officer he had once praised. Montgomery had served as accuser, judge, jury, and executioner. Stephens had little sympathy for anyone who would run away from the war against slavery, but he wondered whether the colonel was "Our active and brave leader" or a Northern slave master.

Twenty-three-year-old Sergeant Henry F. Steward, a farmer from Adrian, Michigan. Wounded during the heroic charge on Fort Wagner on July 18, 1863, Steward died two months later. No photos of Stephens exist, but he would have worn the same uniform and stripes as Steward.

CHAPTER SEVEN
PAYMASTER'S WAGON

Four months of being a soldier and not one cent from the army. With every mail call came pleading letters for money. Families were desperate. Wives and mothers had stretched the state's $50 bounty as far as possible and then beyond. They had to turn to churches, neighbors, or other family members. And some, to their soldier-husband's great shame, had to move into the poorhouses, town institutions for people unable to support themselves.

Earlier in March at Camp Meigs, Gooding had told readers, "We are all determined to act like men, and fight, money or not." He was no longer sure if that was true. To his relief, on the afternoon of June 30, a small wagon arrived, pulled by two mules and flanked by a squad of guards—the paymaster's wagon!

The wagon creaked and its wheels crunched over the sunbaked sand of St. Helena Island, off the coast of South Carolina. The sound held every soldier's attention. Anxious eyes followed the wagon until it stopped in front of the Fifty-Fourth's headquarters.

The paymaster climbed down and went inside. Guards pressed their horses closer to the wagon with its lockbox of crisp bills.

In a matter of minutes, Gooding and a thousand soldiers and officers brushed sand from their pants, wiped the tips of their boots on the back of their pant legs, checked the buttons of their jackets, and scrambled into formation.

Itching in his wool uniform and flannel shirt, Gooding imagined Ellen's smile when the money he would send arrived. But after an hour standing and sweating in the South Carolina heat, he began to worry.

Abraham Lincoln's secretary of war, Edwin Stanton, Massachusetts governor John Andrew, and Frederick Douglass had pledged that Black soldiers would receive the same pay as Whites. Recruiting posters called "TO COLORED MEN" and promised "PAY, $13 A MONTH!"

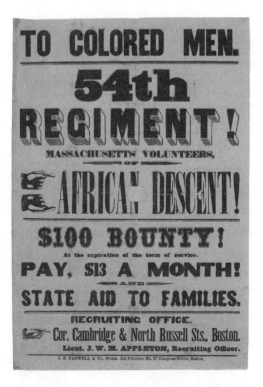

Hundreds of recruiting posters appeared in Black communities throughout the North promising equal pay, $13 a month.

Twenty-year-old Private Abraham Brown from Toronto, Canada. Following the charge on Fort Wagner, Brown accidentally shot himself while cleaning his weapon. He died the next day. No photos of Gooding exist, but he would have worn the same uniform as Brown.

But when Colonel Shaw and the paymaster came out of the plantation house used as headquarters, it was clear something had gone wrong. They were offered $10, not $13. The bad news sank further. Three dollars would be deducted each month for their uniforms.

Regardless of rank or risk, Private Gooding would be paid $7 and White privates $13. White sergeants received $17, but Stephens $7. Black soldiers regardless of rank would be paid $6 less than the lowest-ranking White.

Congress set the army pay for African Americans as laborers, not soldiers. *The New York World* justified the policy, arguing it would be "unjust in every way to the white soldier to put him on a level with the black."

In spite of struggling families at home, the men refused to be paid. And Stephens warned there would be trouble if their pay were not equal. "Do you think that we will tamely submit like spaniels to every indignity?" Gooding's wife, Ellen, and the families of Massachusetts soldiers received state aid. But Stephens and the majority of the Fifty-Fourth came from other states, and because they were not legal residents of Massachusetts their families were not eligible.

"Our enlistment itself is fraudulent," Stephens howled. He felt tricked. He had volunteered for three years in an army that took him hundreds of miles from home and plunked him down on a South Carolina island. And he felt trapped in enemy territory, where Confederates would hang him for being a soldier and the Union refused to pay him as a soldier but would shoot him for not behaving like one.

His sense of betrayal grew deeper with rumors that the War Department planned to give them different color uniforms and replace their rifles with pikes—long poles with sharp iron blades at the point and on the sides. Not since the Middle Ages, four hundred years earlier, had pikes been used in war. But someone in the War Department thought it best if Black soldiers fought with long, sharp poles against an enemy armed with rifles and cannons. Stephens wondered, was it because pikes were like African spears, or was it a plan to annihilate African American soldiers?

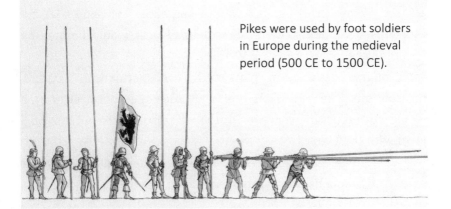

Pikes were used by foot soldiers in Europe during the medieval period (500 CE to 1500 CE).

CHAPTER EIGHT
DARK HEROES

In July, the Fifty-Fourth camped on St. Helena, one island away from Hilton Head and the headquarters of the Union Army's Department of the South. Thousands of soldiers and tons of supplies arrived daily on St. Helena Island. Rumors as thick as mosquitoes filled the air: a major attack on the forts guarding Charleston would soon be launched.

During the day, Stephens, Gooding, and the other Fifty-Fourth soldiers loaded and unloaded ships and, like packhorses, carried supplies back and forth to White regiments camped about the island. In the evenings Shaw drilled them in full uniforms in spite of the heat and humidity. The colonel was determined to show other officers that his Fifty-Fourth was better disciplined and trained than the actions they were ordered to carry out in Darien. Shaw treated them as if they were new recruits back at Camp Meigs, threatening to punish anyone for talking after bedtime and to shoot any guard found sleeping while on duty.

But after six weeks of toting and drilling, Stephens had no reason to believe the Fifty-Fourth would take part in any fighting. And he wasn't surprised when all White regiments were moved to James or Morris Islands, closer to Charleston. The Fifty-Fourth remained on St. Helena, loading and unloading during the day, and drilling in the sticky evening air until bedtime.

Whatever Gooding might have thought, he kept to himself. He simply told his readers, "Instead of going on another expedition, as we all expected and hoped, we find ourselves at the headquarters of the department." But for Stephens, the drudgery of dirt, sand, and sweat was punishment for insisting on equal pay.

The army owed them four months of back pay. If everyone in the regiment were paid $13, that meant $52 per soldier and $52,000 for the 1,000-man regiment. But the army's offer of $7 a month added up to $28 for each soldier, or $28,000 for the regiment. Cheated out of $24,000, the Fifty-Fourth felt they had no choice but to refuse any pay, regardless of the pleas from home. As he calculated the lost money, Stephens felt torn between wanting to fight without pay and fearing he would never have a fair chance. Boxes of pikes would soon arrive and his unused Enfield rifle would be taken away. It drove Stephens to cry out: "Is there no justice in America?"

Shaw no longer reported to Montgomery, but to Brigadier General George Crockett Strong. And he wrote the general asking for a chance for the Fifty-Fourth to serve alongside White soldiers. Shaw wanted to show that his soldiers could do more than carry supplies. General Strong, impressed with any officer who wanted to send his troops into battle, approved Shaw's request and ordered the Fifty-Fourth to James Island.

On July 15, three companies of the Fifty-Fourth, along with White soldiers from the Tenth Connecticut Infantry, stood as early-warning sentinels, or pickets. What Shaw wanted came in the empty space between 4:00 a.m. and dawn. Rising like ground fog, waves of drab-coated rebels came running and yelling like demons released from hell.

During the night the Confederates had maneuvered four large field cannons, called Napoleons, to the edge of the river. The big guns' twelve-pound balls repeatedly hit the Union gunship *Pawnee*, sending sailors and splintered wood into the air. The damaged ship pulled anchor and lumbered downriver, unable to support the men on shore. The Napoleons swiveled and aimed at the pickets and fired.

No amount of drilling could have prepared Stephens for the real-life drama that unfolded. Having fired only in practice, his hands shook as he fumbled for his cartridge box, cap pouch, and ramrod, and held his rifle steady enough to aim and shoot at the screaming demons that kept rising out of the ground. Hundreds and hundreds moved in a gray tidal wave, firing rifles as they advanced.

The Connecticut regiment was trapped. With a swamp at their backs and the Stono River curving from the left and to their front, Stephens and the Fifty-Fourth pickets held a gap that happened to be the only way out. Pickets were expected to hurry back to the main body and join a defensive line once an attack began. But these pickets stayed to cover the Tenth. According to Stephens, when ordered to withdraw they did so "slowly and reluctantly, delivering their fire as if on a skirmish drill."

Stephens aimed, fired, reloaded; aimed again, fired again, reloaded again. Each time his hand moved faster from pouch to teeth as he ripped the paper cartridges and dumped the powder and bullet into his rifle barrel. There was no time to worry about using just one finger to ram a ball into place: the rebels were coming too fast, and men around him were dropping even faster. He slammed his rifle butt against the ground and hoped the ball was in deep enough before he fired. They kept the rebels at bay with their rapid fire, causing unexpected casualties and providing time for most of the Connecticut men to escape the deadly snare. "The rebels yelled and hooted, but they could not drive us, and advanced only as our picket line retired," Stephens would later tell readers.

But a few soldiers of the Fifty-Fourth didn't hear the order to withdraw and were soon surrounded. Ordered to surrender, they kept firing until they fell. One private, however, could no longer take the terror and threw down his rifle; but before he could raise his arms he was shot dead.

The *Pawnee*, meanwhile, had safely steamed downriver and turned its guns on the Confederates. A two-hour artillery duel raged, until the rebel forces withdrew with heavy losses.

Stephens, who had survived his first firefight, let his readers know about the bravery of the Fifty-Fourth. "Every man that fell, fell fighting with his face to the foe."

The *Reflector*, a Connecticut newspaper, likewise celebrated the Fifty-Fourth's success: "The boys of the Tenth Connecticut could not help loving the men who saved them from destruction. . . . [P]robably a thousand homes from Windham to Fairfield have in letters been told the story how the dark-skinned heroes fought the good fight and covered with their own brave hearts the retreat of brothers, sons, and fathers of Connecticut."

Gooding, who was kept back as part of the defensive line, told his readers, "At last we have something stirring to record." After telling of how well the Fifty-Fourth fought, he guessed the cost of that success: "nine killed, 13 wounded, and 17 missing."

Discussions in the War Department about issuing different uniforms and pikes to African American soldiers stopped after the Fifty-Fourth's battle on James Island.

While the "dark-skinned heroes" fought their first battle and saved the Tenth Connecticut, White men in New York City were in their third day of a four-day riot.

Just a few months earlier, the federal government had passed the Enrollment Act, a military draft or conscription measure. It required all army-aged White men, both citizens and immigrants, to register for the army. Their names went into a lottery box, and

From July 13–16, 1863, New York City was the scene of one of the bloodiest anti-Black, anti-draft riots during the Civil War. One historian called it a Confederate victory. An estimated 120 African Americans were killed and millions of dollars in property was destroyed, including the Colored Orphan Asylum where Henry Gooding grew up.

whoever's name was drawn was drafted into the army. The rich could beat the draft by paying $300 or hiring a substitute. Poor and mostly Catholic immigrants lacked the money to buy their way out of the army, and they resented wealthy Protestants who could. The immigrants also detested being forced to risk their lives to liberate slaves, who when freed would move north and, for lower wages, take their jobs.

On July 13, 1863, this poisonous mix of unfairness, class and religious tension, and ethnic hatred boiled over. A large mob overran New York City's draft office on Third Avenue, smashing its windows and setting it ablaze. The mob grew quickly and violence escalated: rioters burned two police stations, beat the police superintendent, cut telegraph lines, and killed trolley horses. At a fever pitch, they turned their anger on Colonel Henry O'Brien, a White officer who had confronted the rioters, and "dragged [him] through the gutters, tortured, shot, and finally hung [him] from a lamppost."

67

What had begun on the morning of July 13 as an anti-draft protest turned into an all-out racial riot. White mobs shouting "Kill the d—d nigger" attacked any Black man, woman, or child found on the streets, and torched buildings where they lived. Victims were beaten to death and hung from lampposts and their bodies were set on fire, or they were drowned in the East River. A mob of several thousand surrounded the Colored Orphan Asylum, where Quaker women had taught and raised Henry Gooding. The rabble chopped through the main door while teachers evacuated 250 children out the back, before the crazed plunderers broke through, looted the orphanage, and burned it to the ground.

The uprising ended when several thousand armed state militia and federal troops occupied the city and restored order. Close to a hundred people were dead, and the city suffered 2.5 million dollars in damage. Two newspapers, the *Daily News* and the *Herald*, blamed the rampage not on the rioters, but on White abolitionists "for fill[ing] the empty heads of the blacks with notions of equality," and for their "zeal for the negro urging him into conspicuous rivalry to white men."

In South Carolina, however, on the afternoon of July 18, the men of the Fifty-Fourth knew nothing of the rioting in New York City. That afternoon they heard only the cheering of 10,000 White soldiers who stepped aside and let them march to the front of the line. Gooding wrote, "We wondered what they were all cheering for, but we soon found out."

CHAPTER NINE

A GRAND CHANCE

Mere hours after the battle on James Island, the Fifty-Fourth received orders to report to General Strong at Morris Island without delay. Without delay was impossible. To get from James Island to the top of Morris Island, at the mouth of Charleston Harbor, would be a battle in itself. And it left the regiment no time to mourn their losses.

The Fifty-Fourth marched throughout the night of Thursday, July 16, in a thunderstorm that "render[ed] the blackness deeper." At times it forced them to squeeze into single file and balance their slimy boots on slippery planks laid across the swamps and mudflats. Pounded by rain and wincing with each bolt of lightning, they moved by "groping their way and grasping their leader as they progressed." Occasionally someone slipped into the marsh and just as quickly scrambled back, before whatever he feared could bite.

At dawn they reached the shoreline, only to face another delay. The transport ship to carry them to Morris Island hadn't arrived. Tired, thirsty, and hungry, they waited until 8:00 that night—and then waited longer. There was one rowboat to carry more than 600 from the shallow waters to the transport ship. They spent the night on the shoreline as thirty men at a time were rowed to the ship.

It wasn't until the next morning, July 18, that the regiment landed and saw the massive earthwork fortress of Fort Wagner, "one of the strongest earthworks ever built."

The fort was a nightmare for any attacking army, stretching across the width of the island's narrow tip—from the edge of the Atlantic Ocean on the eastern side to a swamp on the western side.

But the Union's strategy to capture Charleston started with Fort Wagner. Knock out its gunners, turn Wagner's guns on Fort Sumter, and then turn Sumter's guns on the remaining batteries, thus clearing a sea path to Charleston. Wagner was the key to Charleston, the city where the Civil War began.

The generals in charge ignored the failure of their first attack on Fort Wagner the week before. The Union Army had suffered casualties of more than 300 men. But this time the generals planned to shell the earthwork fort into fine-grained sand and then unleash thousands of soldiers upon the stunned survivors.

General Strong, pleased with the Fifty-Fourth's success on James Island, requested that the Fifty-Fourth be part of the Wagner assault. Two higher-ranking generals whispered to each other: "Well I guess we will let Strong put those d—d negroes from Massachusetts in the advance, we may as well get rid of them, one time as another."

Shaw was offered the chance to lead the charge on Fort Wagner. His men were tired and spent. An officer described their condition: "We were on the move [for] three days and nights" and "were very much exhausted, tired and hungry, not having any thing to eat for twenty four hours." But to Shaw this was an opportunity to erase any doubts about Black soldiers' courage, or at least any doubts about his regiment. He accepted the challenge. It was a "grand chance . . . the one chance which above all others seemed essential!"

The shelling of Wagner started in the afternoon and continued until evening. Nine thousand shells fired at Wagner did little damage except pockmark the ground with deep ditches for attacking soldiers to run around in and be exposed to more fire, or run in and out of to reach Wagner's outer walls. The shelling that General Strong was confident would pulverize the fort and its defenders' will to fight resulted in eight killed and twenty wounded, leaving 1,700 unharmed Confederates sheltered in bombproof mini-caves.

All afternoon the Fifty-Fourth watched the artillery fire as shell after shell smacked into Wagner's earth-and-timber walls. They instinctively ducked when each round hit, yet hoped it would render the fort's soldiers weak and frightened.

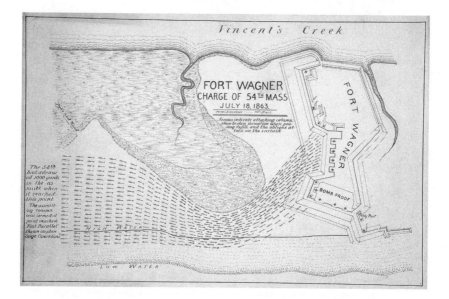

The map shows where the land narrowed and forced the Fifty-Fourth into a tighter mass, making them a more exposed target.

Lewis Douglass was the regiment's first sergeant major. He resigned in 1864 after falling ill with typhus. His father, the famous abolitionist Frederick Douglass, had recruited Lewis and his brother Charles to the Fifty-Fourth.

Around six in the evening, a grim-faced Shaw moved the Fifty-Fourth to the launch point. They passed through thirteen cheering and clapping regiments of White soldiers. Stephens's natural instincts led him to distrust the cheering. Staring at the fort and knowing "of the previous attempt to take it by storm," he "knew that nothing but hard fighting, with great sacrifice of life, could result in a successful storming of it."

As the weary men waited on the beach, Strong galloped toward them, and with his back to the fort, he rallied the men. "I am sorry you must go into the fight tired and hungry, but the men in the fort are tired too. There are but three hundred behind those walls. . . . Don't fire a musket on the way up, but go in and bayonet them at their guns."

Strong pointed to the color-bearer, the man carrying the American flag, and asked, "If this man should fall, who will lift the flag and carry it on?"

There was no immediate answer until Shaw spoke: "I will." He smiled as his soldiers applauded. A prayer-like hush replaced the clapping as they moved within a thousand yards of the fort, capped their rifles, fixed bayonets, and rested.

At 7:40 in the evening, after eleven hours of thunderous siege, the Union shelling stopped. Confederate gunners ran to their artillery pieces, yanked sandbags from the barrels, and dropped in loads of grapeshot— wads of metal balls and shrapnel that spread out like shotgun pellets. Infantrymen fixed bayonets and sprinted to their positions, peered down into the ditches filled with seawater, and readied themselves to shoot anyone who made it out of the ditches alive.

The frantic activity inside the fort contrasted with the calmness a thousand yards away. A somber stillness settled over the island as the group of weary Black soldiers huddled on the beach, their faces masked in a mixture of fear and determination.

With quivering lips Shaw told them how he wanted them to take the fort. "Move in quick time until within a hundred yards of the fort; then double quick, and charge!"

Gooding stared in silence at Wagner, or down at the sand, or the ocean, anywhere but at the other men. He now understood too well why the regiments had cheered when the Fifty-Fourth took their place at the front of the line.

Then the moment came.

They were ordered to their feet and told again, move in quick time until within 100 yards of the fort; then double quick, and charge.

A minute later, Shaw gave the command everyone expected but no one wanted to hear:

"FORWARD!"

CHAPTER TEN
DEAR OLD FLAG

Forward! The command echoed through the regiment, and the men bit their lips and moved toward Fort Wagner. "It was about 7:45 P.M., with darkness coming on rapidly," but each soldier knew that rifle and cannon fire would soon light the evening sky.

Stephens set the pace for B Company as they pushed toward Wagner.

Gooding, with rifle high and bayonet shaking, moved as ordered.

This was the moment they wanted—to "get at the throat of treason and slavery" and prove they were men and soldiers equal to other men and soldiers.

But under a snapping red Confederate flag with its thirteen stars, hundreds of soldiers, some of them just boys, waited with ready rifles and eager fingers. The editor of the *Savannah Morning News* and one of the designers of the Confederate flag, William Thompson, told readers their flag would be "hailed by the civilized world as THE WHITE MAN'S FLAG."

The Fifty-Fourth Regiment became famous for the bravery of the men and officers who made this frontal attack on Fort Wagner.

The riflemen set their sights on a slender White officer waving a sword and the Black soldier running beside him with the Stars and Stripes. But they held their fire and let them lead hundreds of sprinting Black soldiers and a sprinkling of White officers closer and closer. Everything they hated about Abraham Lincoln's North raced toward them.

The gray-coated soldiers inside Fort Wagner could not know the difficulties the blue-coated men below had faced for the chance to charge this fort: their right to be soldiers questioned, their courage doubted, and their pay docked. But on Saturday evening, July 18, 1863, the Fifty-Fourth Massachusetts Infantry charged into the mouths of cannons to erase the past and shape the future they wanted.

On the right flank, Stephens kept his company on pace as he sloshed through the incoming tide. To his left, in the middle of the regiment, Gooding, Sergeant Carney, and C Company jogged on hard-packed sand.

In front, Shaw waved his sword wildly lest the men hesitate under the red-streaked sky. At 100 yards from the fort, all hell broke loose as the Confederate shooters opened fire. One survivor wrote, "they mowed us down like grass." Bags of grapeshot spun through the charging regiment, and a thousand rifles pushed a wall of bullets into the mass of blue-coated men, who fell in screaming agony. "Mortal men could not stand such fire," Gooding said.

Shaw kept running; the soldier with the flag kept pace, as did Gooding, Stephens, and those still able to follow. They went in and out of seawater-filled ditches, through the storm of bullets and

Carney became the first Black Medal of Honor recipient for his bravery at Fort Wagner.

spinning grapeshot, until they reached Wagner's low parapet, or wall. Shaw climbed up and stood waving his sword, shouting again and again, "Come on, men! Follow me!"

Shaw's silver colonel's eagles and strained pale face were a tempting target, but the rebels let him lead more soldiers into killing range. And when they were close enough, a new wall of fire erupted. The color-bearer slumped to the ground; the Stars and Stripes dropped beside him.

True to his word, Shaw bent to pick up the flag. But he was unable to come fully to his feet as bullet after bullet struck him, until he pitched forward. "When the men saw their gallant leader fall, they made a desperate effort to get him out, but they were either shot down, or reeled in the ditch below," Gooding later told readers.

Sergeant Carney threw down his rifle, picked up the flag, and planted it where Shaw had fallen to help others see a way into the fort.

Gooding, who had missed the burning of Darien and the fighting on James Island, summoned the courage needed to survive. He slid inside the fort and fired one round. And with no time or room to reload, he jabbed his bayonet at whoever came at him, and when they were too close he used the rifle butt as a club. While shooting, stabbing, and clubbing, he prayed for reinforcements.

Stephens found his way inside the fort, and after firing once used his bayonet and rifle butt to fight until the rifle stock snapped and splintered in his hands. He too prayed for the second wave of Union soldiers to come and help.

Help came. Men from Third New Hampshire Regiment poured into the hellishly darkened space but were quickly overwhelmed by the screams of the dying and the fiendish hand-to-hand slaughter. Unable to tell friend from foe, they fired at anything that moved. "[T]hey, to a man, emptied their rifles into us," Stephens wrote. "Thus we lost nearly as many men by the bullets of our presumed friends as by those of our known enemies."

General Strong had no choice but to call a retreat. The Confederates, pleased to see a Union general within range, made sure it was his last order: Strong fell, mortally wounded. A few moments later, Colonel Putnam, leader of the second wave, who had warned they were going in like sheep to the slaughter, received a shot to the head and a quick death.

Errors and chaos continued. Guards left behind to prevent men from "skedaddling," or running away, had started drinking early that afternoon, and by 9:00 they were drunk. They started shooting the retreating soldiers. Finally, a wounded officer of the Fifty-Fourth, witnessing his sergeant being shot, pulled his own pistol and killed one of the drunks. Only then did the guard detachment shake off its alcoholic haze.

The lucky and uninjured made it out of the fort blazing with enemy and friendly fire, and past the drunken guards, to safety. Gooding was one of those blessed with such luck, as was Stephens, but without his rifle.

Hours later, Sergeant Carney, with chest and arm wounds, crawled into camp using just one arm, carrying the flag under the other. He is credited with saying that the "dear old flag" never touched the ground. And perhaps Carney did say those exact words, which soon appeared in stories of the battle. But there is no doubt that he exposed himself by standing on the wall of Fort Wagner as a beacon for soldiers to follow, or that he crawled on hand and knees to bring the national colors back. For those actions Carney became the first African American awarded the Medal of Honor, the military's highest honor, for valor above and beyond the call of duty.

Others wounded were not as fortunate. Unable even to crawl, many drowned in the rising tide around Fort Wagner. Of the 624 men of the Fifty-Fourth who charged Wagner, 54 were killed, 149 were wounded, and 76 were taken prisoner; almost half of the regiment was lost in less than two hours. White officers were especially prized targets: only one returned alive or uninjured. Colonel Shaw fell on the walls of Wagner; Captains Simpkins and Russel of K and H Companies died next to each other on the field. Russel was three days shy of his nineteenth birthday.

On Sunday morning, July 19, Confederates believed they were adding a final insult to a White officer leading Black soldiers. Laws and customs in both the North and the South prohibited burial of Whites and Blacks in the same cemetery. The rebel burial detail "stripped" Colonel Robert Gould Shaw's body "of all his clothing save under-vest and drawers" and tossed him facedown in a trench. Twenty of his men were thrown on top of him, and their mass grave covered in South Carolina sand. As a Confederate officer put it: "Had he been in command of white troops, I should have given him an honorable burial; as it is, I shall bury him in the common trench with his negroes that fell with him."

CHAPTER ELEVEN

ARE WE SOLDIERS?

Men were going to die, reasoned Quincy Gillmore and Truman Seymour, the top generals, so it didn't matter which regiment, Black or White, led the charge.

For Colonel Shaw, it had been a "grand chance" for his Black regiment to show they were as brave as any.

For Stephens, Gooding, and the soldiers of the Fifty-Fourth, it was the opportunity to prove they were equal to Whites and should be treated the same as White soldiers.

No matter how it was justified, they all paid dearly. Bayonets drawn, Shaw and the Fifty-Fourth had charged into the mouths of cannons. On that July evening, there'd been no glory. Soldiers were dead or writhing in agony from wounds, or—worse, some thought—soldiers were captured and taken into Charleston's jail to be punished as slaves who had conspired to kill their masters.

The casualties numbered more than 200. And after all the bravery, blood, and loss, Fort Wagner still stood. Its flag flapped over the fort, and gray-coated soldiers slunk behind sand and timber walls with rifles and cannons poised for the next suicidal charge.

Two days later a siege, a slow-moving assault to squeeze the life out of Wagner, began. Gooding, the corporals, and the privates dug what the army called sap lines. Soldiers carved crisscrossing trenches toward the fort and pulled and shoved their heavy artillery guns forward. They inched hour by hour, while rebel sharpshooters picked, at will, which life to end. It became "an ordinary spectacle to see stretchers passing, with blood trickling through the canvass [sic]," Gooding wrote. The unnerving sounds of burial fifes became commonplace, but never so ordinary that soldiers didn't pause in mid-shovel.

For the soldiers to make progress, the burial fifes were ordered to stop. The digging carried on. And the Fifty-Fourth had sharpshooters of their own. From July 20 to September 6, day and night, seven days a week in eight-hour shifts, the regiment etched deep trenches across the sandy ground.

While Gooding dug, Stephens and other sergeants of the Fifty-Fourth acted as officers and directed the digging. Only one officer, E Company's Captain Luis F. Emilio, had survived the assault uninjured. Stephens believed the War Department would have to drop its ban on African American officers. With only one officer, the Fifty-Fourth needed more commissioned leaders. The big prizes of Fort Sumter and Charleston, where the war had started, had yet to fall.

Even when news of the New York City Draft Riots reached the Fifty-Fourth, Stephens hoped that the War Department would drop its ban on Black officers. New officers were needed. Although Stephens wanted a promotion, he did not hide his outrage about the murderous riots. In August, he sent a thunderbolt to his *Anglo-African* readers: "mob-fiends upheld the assassin knife, and brandished the incendiary torch over the heads of our wives and children to burn their homes, [while] we were doing our utmost to sustain the honor of our country's flag."

Gooding, on the other hand, reacted in silence. He did not write a word about the burning of the orphanage where he had lived. And though he may have felt it, he did not express concern for his former teachers, some of whom saved 250 children from a mob that held Black orphans responsible for the war. Gooding could not acknowledge the pain caused by his former enslavement. He chose to keep his past secret.

Nothing had stopped the sap lines from crawling forward. After forty-nine days of sweat, grit, and blood, the soldiers of the Fifty-Fourth inched within seventy-five yards of the fort and fired artillery to pulverize it. At 2:00 a.m. on September 7, 1863, the Fifty-Fourth lined up for another charge—but the order to advance never came. The Confederates had abandoned the fort during the night. Stephens could at last write, "*Mr. Editor:* Fort Wagner has fallen!"

Gooding ventured inside the destroyed fort to better describe their success. He quickly became overwhelmed and horrified by what he found. "The smell in Wagner is really sickening; dead men and mules are profuse, some exposed to the rays of sun, and others being half buried by earth thrown over them by our shot and shell during the bombardment."

The Confederacy suffered 186 casualties defending the fort. The Union sacrificed 1,854 lives to capture it and move a mile closer to Charleston.

Before this, on August 7, nineteen days into the siege, the soldiers of the Fifty-Fourth had once again stood in front of the paymaster's wagon. For the second time, regardless of rank, they were offered $10 a month minus $3 for uniforms, instead of the $13 White soldiers received for taking the same risks. Colonel Montgomery's Second Carolina accepted the $10. But when the Fifty-Fourth was asked, "All who wished to take the ten dollars per month, raise your hand," Gooding proudly told readers, "I am glad to say not one man in the whole regiment lifted a hand." He concluded in his letter to the *New Bedford Mercury*: "Too many of our comrades' bones lie bleaching near the walls of Fort Wagner to subtract even one <u>cent</u> from our hard earned pay."

Stephens dismissed the payment as "insulting" to be offered "about half the pay of a poor white private."

Seven weeks later, tired of waiting for equal compensation, Gooding brushed the dirt from his pants and hands to keep from smudging his writing paper and sat outside his tent with a wood plank across his lap. He wrote to Abraham Lincoln. He began timidly, "Your Excellency," and begged to be pardoned for "the presumption of a humble individual." But his writing grew stronger as he continued.

He asked, "Are we <u>Soldiers</u>, or are we <u>Labourers</u>?" Gooding reminded Lincoln that even though the African American had for two years been refused "the privilege of aiding his Country in her need," this day "he is in the War, and how has he conducted himself? Let their dusky forms rise up, out [of] the mires of James Island, and give the answer. Let the rich mould around Wagner's parapets be upturned, and there will be found an Eloquent answer." As his passion grew, he challenged: "Now your Excellency, we have done a Soldier's Duty. Why Can't we have a Soldier's pay?"

A White New York reporter had been covering the war on Morris Island. Gooding asked him to mail the letter to President Lincoln. He did not want the letter read by the army or the War Department. Letters to the president and commander-in-chief were expected to be approved by the regimental commander, then by the Union Army's Department of the South, and finally the War Department. Only then if all censors approved the letter would it be sent to the White House. Gooding violated the army's chain of command and dreaded that if caught he would end up bucked and gagged, or worse.

On September 30, after the siege, the paymaster returned a third time. Although penniless and with suffering families at home, the Fifty-Fourth refused to accept anything less than full pay. When Colonel James Montgomery heard of their third rejection, he stormed into camp and ordered the men to assemble. Dressed in full uniform, soldiers fell into formation and waited as the old colonel let them stew in the sticky South Carolina heat. Sweat trickled under Stephens's woolen uniform and rolled down to his socks.

Montgomery at last began, "I am your friend," but quickly used the word "nigger" twice. Forgetting or ignoring the fact that he was speaking to free men who had willingly risked their lives and freedom and come South to fight, he said, "A great many of you are fugitive slaves, and can by law be returned to your masters. The government by its act in setting you free has paid you a thousand dollars bounty." They "ought to be glad," he said, "to pay for the privilege to fight, instead of squabbling for money."

Gooding's September 28, 1863, letter to Abraham Lincoln in which he asks, "Why Can't we have a Soldier's pay?"

Stephens and the rest of the regiment stood rigid. To move or relax their stance, to show any sign of disrespect, would be an excuse to be shot. But not reacting became harder as Montgomery told them the only way they could be "placed on the same footing as white soldiers" was by being "as good soldiers as the white." And they were after all, he said, only a race of slaves whose fathers a few years ago "worshipped snakes and crocodiles in Africa."

Toward the end of his hour-long rant, Montgomery switched to insulting their appearance: "Your features can be improved. Your beauty cannot recommend you. Your yellow faces are evidences of rascality. You should get rid of this bad blood. My advice to you is the lightest of you must marry the blackest women." His words stung Stephens, Gooding, and the other mixed-race soldiers, who knew their complexions came from White fathers or grandfathers who had fathered them with the Black women they owned. It was this "bad blood" Montgomery wanted them to somehow be rid of.

The colonel's rage ended with a threat. If they did not accept the $7, they would be guilty of insubordination and mutiny. And Montgomery reminded them "mutiny is punishable with death." No one showed any disrespect to Colonel Montgomery, but each soldier became more determined not to accept anything less than full and equal pay.

In a long letter to the publisher of the *Anglo African*, Stephens's calm, well-chosen words laid bare the fallacy of Montgomery's thinking. Stephens wrote, "As to yellow faces I don't indulge in any controversy about color. I think 'tis the mind that makes the man,' not the color of his skin or any peculiarity of his hair. All I wish to know is the man just, is he humane and generous—noble-spirited—if yes, he is a man, if no, he is a slave to passion and iniquity."

Letters and visits from soldiers, their families, and supporters of the Fifty-Fourth poured into Governor Andrew's office. The governor, an abolitionist and champion of social equality, worried the soldiers would think he had tricked them, rather than understanding that he himself had been deceived by the War Department. He persuaded his state legislature to make up the $6-a-month difference. In December 1863, the governor's representatives traveled to South Carolina with $54,000—only to be shocked when the Fifty-Fourth refused to accept it. The soldiers insisted on full pay from the federal government, not charity from Massachusetts. If the War Department paid them in full, the Black soldiers would be considered equal to White soldiers.

Gooding had been promoted to corporal on December 5. He disagreed with the regiment's decision, though he did not say so publicly. He believed the men had gone too far in not accepting the governor's offer. Every week, one or more among the soldiers received a letter telling of desperate need at home to pay rent or buy food. Gooding worried that the growing anger and distrust would soon explode and destroy the Fifty-Fourth. He took it upon himself to fix the problem, and did what he did best—turned to pen and paper.

Gooding assumed the self-appointed role of a wise man, interpreting African American thinking to the governor. He wrote of an approaching crisis over pay and offered to "avert it before it assumes a larger shape." He explained that "the men of the regiment do not <u>understand</u> the terms of the Governor's message." They were carrying the matter "too far" by claiming that Massachusetts' making up the $6 difference was supporting the War Department's "injustice."

Gooding wrote that the Massachusetts offer had been rejected because "[t]he African race are naturally suspicious, arising from ignorance." And he advised the governor to send his offer directly to each man, "say a thousand copies," in simple language, so "they may know that the State means to do justly, not act to please their vanity or dignity."

Gooding wanted to make sure that the army and War Department did not see his letter, so he did not write directly to the governor. Instead, he sent his letter to James Bunker Congdon, the New Bedford banker he knew from his work with New Bedford's Anti-Slavery Society. Congdon thought well of Gooding and knew

Governor Andrew. Gooding asked Congdon to mail the letter from New Bedford to the governor.

Governor Andrew did receive the letter. He may have frowned in surprise at Gooding's description of his fellow soldiers' suspicion arising from ignorance rather than principle. The governor did not respond to Gooding, but he told Congdon the decision not to pay soldiers equally was a "mistake in law, as well as in justice and policy."

As 1863 came to a close, Fort Sumter and Charleston lay in the distance, unconquered. More than a third of the Fifty-Fourth soldiers who had marched out of Boston six months previously had been lost. Those alive were still without pay. Gooding worried about his letters. Had they reached the president or the governor, or had they been intercepted by the War Department? New officers had also joined the regiment. All White. No one from the regiment had been promoted to a commissioned officer, leaving Stephens to wait for the day when that would change.

But these worries and frustrations were put on hold. In January 1864, the regiment sailed from South Carolina to Florida. Neither Stephens nor Gooding had any idea why.

CHAPTER TWELVE
THREE CHEERS

On February 8, 1864, Corporal James Henry Gooding wrote from Jacksonville, Florida, "[W]e were off on another tramp, but with no knowledge of our destination," and he closed with an optimistic flourish, "no strenuous opposition as yet."

Early Saturday morning, February 20, almost a year after Gooding left New Bedford to join the Fifty-Fourth, he marched with his regiment on a sandy road in Florida. The previous day they had marched eighteen miles from Jacksonville, and they had left camp at Baldwin shortly after breakfast. Their route ran parallel to the Atlantic & Gulf Central Railroad. Without knowing it, Gooding and the Fifty-Fourth were part of a plan "to restore Florida to her allegiance."

After nearly three years of fighting, Northern support for the Civil War and emancipation had plunged. High casualty rates combined with too few victories made Abraham Lincoln's chances for reelection in November doubtful. The Fifty-Fourth was part of a force of 5,000 Union soldiers heading for Tallahassee, Florida's state capital. Along the way they were to free slaves and capture Confederate soldiers. Freed slaves old enough to carry a rifle would be forced into the Union Army, and White prisoners would be given a choice between signing a loyalty oath and returning home without their weapons, or spending the rest of the war in a Northern prison camp. If 10 percent of White men (only White men could vote) claimed loyalty to the United States, Florida would be readmitted to the Union, which would improve President Lincoln's reelection chances.

Colonel Ned Hallowell, formerly Shaw's second in command, had recovered from his Fort Wagner wound and returned to take charge of the Fifty-Fourth. But with Shaw and General Strong dead, the Massachusetts regiment was once again assigned to Colonel James Montgomery's "colored brigade," now made up of the First North Carolina Colored Volunteers and the Fifty-Fourth.

Stephens, after months of digging sap lines and dodging sniper bullets at Wagner, put aside his distrust of Montgomery. As they headed west for the state capital he joined Gooding and the rest of the regiment in singing, "We're bound for Tallahassee in the morning."

Around two in the afternoon, seven hours into the march, near the town of Olustee, Florida, Gooding heard the first shots of a coming battle. Held in reserve to be used only if necessary, the men of the Fifty-Fourth halted and watched more than 4,000 Union soldiers move forward to meet the enemy. Gooding found shade under a tall pine tree and smiled as some of the men listening to the roar of artillery and the faint sounds of rifle fire hid their anxiety in morbid banter:

"That's home-made thunder," one of them joked.

"I don't mind the thunder if the lightning don't strike me!" said another.

But shortly after 3:30 they were sent running into that thunder and lightning to hold off the Confederates as defeated Union soldiers retreated. Gooding, in one of his first duties as a corporal, was given color guard duty and ran next to and guarded Corporal Henry Peal, who carried the Massachusetts state flag. The two of them led the Fifty-Fourth toward the gunfire. As their pace picked up, soldiers threw off their knapsacks and someone shouted, "Three cheers for Massachusetts and seven dollars a month!"

Montgomery and the North Carolina soldiers followed several yards behind. The closer to the fighting, the more the road clogged with a disordered mass of wounded and stragglers who cried out in shock, "We're badly whipped!" and "You'll all get killed."

The battle was fought on flat spongy ground with green clumps of hemlock bushes and pine trees tall and thin as candlesticks. Gooding took a position behind one of the trees as other soldiers frantically searched for something better. While Gooding fired at the advancing rebels, Stephens swung B Company into battle-line formation against what he described later as "a stupendous ambuscade."

A *New York Times* reporter watching the Union withdrawal observed: "The two colored regiments had stood in the gap and saved the army." The Fifty-Fourth protected the left flank of the retreating soldiers. And the North Carolina men covered the right, but after taking heavy fire that cost them 230 men, they fell back. Suddenly the Fifty-Fourth stood alone, fully exposed, with no way to withdraw—six hundred African Americans from the North in the direct path of thousands of Southern White infantry and cavalry. That very morning, an officer of the Second Florida Cavalry had told his men that Black soldiers were "here to steal, pillage, run over the state and murder, kill, and rape our wives, daughters, and sweethearts. Let's teach them a lesson. I shall not take any negro prisoners in this fight."

Outnumbered five to one, and with no order to withdraw,

the Fifty-Fourth had been either forgotten or sacrificed. Under a withering fire, Stephens saw Sergeant Major Stephen Swails fall as he returned to the line after delivering a report to Colonel Hallowell. But Stephens did not see Corporal Peal fall dead on top of the state flag, or see Gooding's surprised look when a bullet caught him in the thigh and he crumpled to the ground.

Confederates poured out from behind their barricade and began to advance. Stephens and the surviving soldiers kept firing round after round as fast as they could reload. Montgomery, who had remained on the field, ordered them to fade into the tall pinewoods and fight their way to safety. "Now, men, you have done well," he bellowed. "I love you all. Each man take care of himself."

In the chaos of artillery shells clipping treetops and bullets hitting men, Colonel Hallowell became separated from the regiment. But his second in command, Lieutenant Colonel Henry Hooper, disobeyed Montgomery and ordered the regiment to stay in place. He formed them as best he could into a line and commanded them to demonstrate the manual of arms.

What appeared as madness slowed the Confederates, who were now 300 yards away. What soldiers, outnumbered as they were, would stop to perform a parade-ground drill? But Hooper wanted to squelch any urge to panic and give his men confidence by having them quickly do a routine exercise. And it worked. The puzzling sight of these "wooly head" soldiers who should have been running for their lives instead of drilling in the middle of a rout caused the rebels to stop, suspicious of being lured into a trap. And it allowed the Fifty-Fourth to take advantage of the confusion and withdraw.

Three hundred yards later they stopped, snapped bayonets in place, and gave nine cheers as if replacements had arrived. After another 300 yards they turned and fired a mass of musket balls that showered the cautiously pursuing Confederates with chunks of pine. They continued their veteran-cool withdrawal for another 300 yards, did a quick about-face with their bayonets shimmering

In this battle, fought on February 20, 1864, the Confederates forced Union troops to retreat back to Jacksonville. The Union suffered heavy casualties. The Fifty-Fourth casualties consisted of 11 killed, 47 wounded, and 8 missing. Corporal James Henry Gooding was first reported killed and later as missing.

in the weak February light, and let fly another volley of shots. A hundred yards later, they spotted the Second Florida Cavalry, whose lieutenant had urged them to take no prisoners. But fearing a trap, the rebel officer would not let his horsemen ride into the darkening woods with an unknown number of bayonets facing them.

The Fifty-Fourth continued another few hundred yards and did a final about-face, to find the piney woods of Olustee now empty of gray-coated hunters.

As they retreated back to Baldwin, Stephens found Sergeant Major Swails on the side of the road, delirious from a head wound. Swails had stumbled this far before collapsing from loss of blood. He was loaded into a wagon that would carry him to the train station at

Sanderson, ten miles away; from there he could be taken to the army field hospital in Jacksonville.

The Fifty-Fourth continued its retreat, carrying some of their wounded with them. Gooding was left behind. Total Union losses were a shocking 1,861. The Confederates lost half as many. The disastrous four-hour Battle of Olustee liberated no slaves and put an immediate end to the White House's secret plan to return Florida to the Union, and Lincoln's chances for reelection spiraled downward as word of the defeat spread across the North.

As his regiment moved to safety, Gooding lay among the bodies that littered the pinewoods. He stayed alive by staunching his wound, enduring the searing pain, and not crying out as gunshots came nearer. As if on a pleasant Sunday stroll, Confederate soldiers searched the fields for wounded Black soldiers and their White officers. Gooding heard the tearful pleadings followed by a gunshot and silence, after which the easy conversation resumed and the rebel soldiers continued their murderous stroll. One Georgia soldier wrote his mother, "I tell you our men slayed the Negrows & if it had not been for the officers their would not one of them been spaired [sic]."

Gooding survived the night of pain and executions. But the next morning, he was discovered by a Confederate officer and taken prisoner.

CHAPTER THIRTEEN

ANDERSONVILLE

 eat and stench choked Gooding as he elbowed for breathing space. Locked inside a dark and airless railroad cattle car with forty or more unwashed prisoners, Gooding feared suffocation. And with each bump over the war-neglected rails, a searing pain shot through his badly injured leg. His tattered trousers did not conceal—from sight, touch, or smell—an oozing, infected battle wound.

White prisoners from the Seventh New Hampshire and the Seventh Connecticut, also captured at Olustee, were dressed in their ragged uniforms, but Gooding and the other Black soldiers were now barefoot and in cast-off slave clothes. Guards had taken their uniforms because they considered them slaves in rebellion, not prisoners of war.

The cattle cars rattled 125 miles from Tallahassee, Florida, to Americus, Georgia. On Monday, March 14, 1864, almost a year after

Gooding had proudly marched out of New Bedford, he reached Camp Sumter Military Prison, called Andersonville, in southwest Georgia.

Townspeople and off-duty guards gathered for their first look at the Black men captured at Olustee. Georgia's Slave Codes spelled out the punishment for a slave who rebelled, or set fire to a house, or taught another slave how to make poison; but the idea of a slave with a gun was so unthinkable that no code had been written for its punishment. The sight of Gooding and other Black soldiers, even out of uniform, filled the small town with alarm and disgust.

Gooding hobbled in agony, helped by other prisoners, as they walked the couple of miles to the prison camp. There they waited in an open field for Captain Henry Wirz, the prison commander, to make his appearance. When he arrived, Wirz was dressed in a crisp white shirt and matching pants, with a large holstered pistol hanging from his narrow waist. His hawkish eyes darted across the field full of his prey. In a heavy Swiss-German accent, he conveyed his single message: obey or perish.

Marched through a large stockade gate, Gooding and twenty others entered a rectangular area with another gate locked in front of them. Slowly the door behind them squeaked closed, and then soldier clerks began demanding names, ranks, and regiments. Gooding's "corporal" and "Massachusetts" met with outright sneers. With the information taken, the second gate squeaked open—and Gooding's shocked heart sank further.

He entered sixteen acres of suffering. Thousands and thousands of vacant-eyed men stood before him, half-starved, listless; none even lifted his head to see the new arrivals. There were no barracks or shelters. Instead, thousands of makeshift tents had been haphazardly pieced together from shreds of blankets, jackets, or rags and fastened over hard-to-find sticks. Those who had nothing at all to sleep under spent their days and nights—rain, heat, or cold—in the open.

Adding to Gooding's shock was the stomach-turning stench of the "sinks," long wooden troughs used as toilets by 13,000 men

Andersonville Prison was crowded with makeshift tents because of the lack of barracks. At the bottom of the photo are the noxious "sinks."

each day. From time to time, piles of human feces were pushed into a marsh that soon became no more than a vast open sewer. Many of the sick and injured could not make it to the sinks and were left to hand-scoop a hole in the ground. The prison had become a petri dish of disease and infection.

Though Black and White prisoners had arrived together, they separated from each other once inside the stockade. Gooding limped to the area near the south gate where the Black soldiers stayed. Of the one hundred African American prisoners, forty-seven had been captured with Gooding at Olustee. Men in both areas spent the day in the blistering sun, with nothing to do and little to eat. At night they slid under their homemade shelters or just lay down where they were, on the filthy ground.

There were no guards inside the stockade, but on the outside walls, every fifty yards, young soldiers stood on "pigeon roosts" in four-hour shifts, day and night, guarding the emaciated prisoners. The guards' main duty was to make sure no one crossed the Dead

Line—a thin rail fence set nineteen feet inside the stockade walls. It marked a no-man's land that kept prisoners from approaching the walls. Gooding soon learned that anyone who ventured beyond the Dead Line—whether to reach for a piece of firewood or by falling down while rushing to the sinks at night—was instantly shot.

Georgia slaves had built the Andersonville prison in just a few weeks, because the North and the South had stopped exchanging prisoners and both sides needed more prisons. Up until the Emancipation Proclamation, a gentlemen's agreement had been in place for returning prisoners of war: privates were exchanged for privates, captains for captains. This practical arrangement saved each side the expense and manpower of guarding and caring for prisoners. But after 1863, when Black soldiers joined the Union Army, the Confederacy refused to exchange the Black prisoners, as it would suggest that they were equal to Whites. The rebels vowed to "die in the last ditch" before "giving up the right to send slaves back to slavery as property recaptured."

Abraham Lincoln directed his army not to exchange rebel prisoners until *all* Union prisoners, regardless of color, would be exchanged. The Confederates refused—and within just months, Northern and Southern prisons were grossly overcrowded. As the cost of feeding, guarding, and housing thousands of men became overwhelming, the Confederates offered a compromise: they would exchange Black prisoners who had been born free, but *not* those who were slaves when the war started. Lincoln refused to accept the distinction; they were *all* Union soldiers.

To relieve the desperate overcrowding, the Confederates needed another prison immediately. They picked the small town of Andersonville, in southwest Georgia, for the new prison, which would hold up to 10,000 men. The town had a good source of clean water in its Sweetwater Creek, and it had a large pine forest nearby for lumber. The railroad in Americus, a few miles away, could

Close to 13,000 Union soldiers died during the fourteen months the prison existed.

transport large quantities of men and supplies. The prison was formally named Camp Sumter Military Prison, though it became better known as just Andersonville.

The first prisoner arrived on February 27, 1864. By the time Gooding arrived two weeks later, Andersonville already held 13,000 prisoners, 3,000 more than it could handle. Captain Wirz soon discovered that although the woods near the prison were full of trees for lumber, there were no nails for building shelters. He also learned that the Confederate Army's need for beef and vegetables was more important than feeding his Union prisoners. Added to Wirz's problems, the camp's freshwater creek turned foul. By June of 1864, just three months after Andersonville had opened, 26,000 sick and starving Union soldiers were caged inside its pine stockade walls. That month, rain fell on twenty-two out of thirty days.

From Camp Meigs in Massachusetts, Gooding had written, "When the war is over, and those who are spared to return shall march through the grand thoroughfares of our principal cities, ragged, lame, shoeless, and a banner tattered and torn by hostile balls, they then will learn who holds the highest place in the affections of a grateful people." But now Gooding languished in Andersonville, without shelter, clean water, adequate food, or medical attention. He was filthy, shoeless, and lame with a festering wound. He also lacked pencil and paper to express either his outrage or his unwavering pride in all he had done.

A White prisoner who kept a secret diary noted "a dozen or more Negroes, all prisoners of war. Nearly all are minus an arm or leg, and their wounds are yet unhealed. Many of them are gangrened and they will all surely die."

After four months in Andersonville, Gooding's wound turned markedly worse. As he neared starvation, his small body shrank, robbing his face of his features. At last his thin brown body could take it no more. On the morning of July 19, 1864, Gooding died.

James Henry Gooding left no words of either rage or praise. Gravediggers carried his body to the dead house, removed his rag clothes and anything useful to the living, and laid him atop the ninety other men who had died that day. Late in the afternoon they carted him to the burial grounds where, without coffin or prayer, they lowered him into a wide trench, side-by-side and shoulder-to-shoulder with White Union soldiers, and covered him in the red dirt of Georgia. Gooding became the 3,585th Union soldier buried at Andersonville.

James Henry Gooding's grave can be seen at Andersonville National Cemetery, Andersonville, Georgia.

CHAPTER FOURTEEN

MUTINY AND HONOR

Four months before Gooding died, the men of the Fifty-Fourth edged toward mutiny. Thirteen months without pay, more than a third of the regiment was dead, wounded, or missing. Enough! Simmering anger boiled over on April 17, 1864. When their transport ship anchored at Folly Island, South Carolina, the soldiers refused to leave the ship. They huddled in small brooding groups, disobeying a direct order from Ned Hallowell, who was now a full colonel. Hallowell repeated the order, but no one moved, including Stephens.

Colonel Hallowell sympathized with the soldiers' struggle for equal pay, but he had army discipline to maintain. He ordered one of his captains aboard. The officer stormed up the gangplank, grabbed the first soldier he reached, and shoved him along. Stephens had no choice but to order his company ashore. They grudgingly followed, but some continued their protest by mumbling, "[M]oney or blood!" or, "[M]uster us out or pay us!"

Being forced off the ship neither quelled the resentment nor eased the sense of betrayal. Instead, it sparked another confrontation. On the morning of May 12, Stephens kept silent as his men protested. Lieutenant Robert Newell, a twenty-one-year-old who had left Harvard to join the Fifty-Fourth following the loss of officers at Fort Wagner, ordered B Company to fall in for morning inspection. Six men remained near their tents and refused. The lieutenant repeated his order, and Stephens, their sergeant, made no effort to help. He considered Newell a fair-minded officer but believed the War Department's policy of allowing only White officers prevented him from being B Company's lieutenant. The lack of pay and blocked promotion led Stephens to stand at attention and let the protest continue.

The men of B Company, including Stephens, respected Lieutenant Newell. But six of them were fed up. The War Department used them as soldiers but wanted to pay them as ditch diggers. Once again they ignored the lieutenant's order.

Soon men from other companies came to watch what the young officer would do. The public challenge to his authority forced Newell to act. He pulled his sword and slapped one man with its flat side, to sting without drawing blood, and repeated his order a fourth time. Again the six refused. Rumors of the standoff traveled through camp, and more men rushed to watch.

Newell, now with revolver in hand, repeated the order a final time. Confident their officer was only bluffing, the soldiers remained by their tents. Newell blinked once and shuddered as he pulled the trigger, shooting one man in the chest. Stunned, the five others scrambled to join B Company's formation. Newell, "white as a sheet," was just as stunned; he had joined the army to fight the Confederates and slavery, not to shoot African American soldiers. He ordered two privates to carry the wounded man to the medical area and hoped the poor man would recover.

Stephens kept his thoughts to himself, stared straight ahead, and silently stood at attention. He was convinced that the lack of

After Robert Gould Shaw's death, Hallowell commanded the Fifty-Fourth. He advocated, as did Shaw, for equal pay, but he went a step further and recommended Blacks as officers.

a chance for promotion and no pay meant the Fifty-Fourth was pressed, as he would write soon afterward, "under a tyranny (as) inexorable as slavery itself."

A full-scale mutiny happened a few miles away in the Fifty-Fifth Massachusetts's camp. The trouble started a few days after Lieutenant Newell shot one of his own soldiers. But it took a month for its deadly consequences to play out.

Lieutenant Thomas F. Ellsworth, recently a sergeant in a White regiment who had transferred to the Fifty-Fifth for the promotion, ordered his company to assemble for inspection. Nineteen-year-old Private Wallace Baker, a sour and sullen freed slave from Tennessee, joined the formation late and without his rifle.

Asked why, Baker replied, "I'm not going to hurry."

Ordered back to his tent for his rifle, Baker refused. "I won't do it, I'll be dammed if I will."

Soldiers in the ranks started to laugh, which in turn drove

Baker to laugh, humiliating the new lieutenant. Ellsworth grabbed Baker by the collar and pushed him toward his tent. Baker knocked his hands away and punched Ellsworth twice in the face, while bellowing, "You damned white officer, do you think that you can strike me, and I not strike you back again? I will do it. I'm damned if I don't."

Ellsworth drew his sword. Baker seized it from him and hit him again. The lieutenant called for help, but not a soldier rushed to the lieutenant's aid. Two other officers arrived and subdued Baker, but when they called for guards to take him away, no one stepped forward. The officers were left to stand alone, with swords and pistols pointing at hundreds of Black soldiers who were fed up with their treatment. The officers marched Baker away to await trial for an offense that had only one form of punishment.

Colonel Alfred Hartwell, commander of the Fifty-Fifth, had no choice but to order Baker's execution. He wrote to Governor Andrew, "For God's sake how long can this injustice of the government be continued toward these men? Are we to goad them into mutiny and [then] quench the mutiny in blood?"

On Friday, June 17, the sentence was carried out. Every soldier on Folly Island was required to watch, including the men of the Fifty-Fourth and Fifty-Fifth. At mid-morning, a mule-drawn wagon guarded by White soldiers carried Private Baker with hands tied behind his back. The guards helped him down from the wagon and placed him between his grave and a firing squad. Every soldier knew the lesson being taught: strike an officer, no matter the reason, and you will be put to a firing squad.

Neither a blindfold, a target pinned to his jacket, nor the chaplain's prayers could stop Baker from cursing the army, the Union, and Abraham Lincoln, until the force of bullets stopped him mid-sentence and slammed his corpse into the waiting grave. A fatigue detail from the Fifty-Fifth gently crossed his arms and closed his eyes before covering him in dirt.

After watching Baker's execution, Stephens took to his own pen and joined in damning Abraham Lincoln. In his August article in the *Anglo-African*, he told thousands of African American readers in the army and at home: "Nearly eighteen months of service—of labor—of humiliation—of danger, and not one dollar. . . . What can wipe the wrong and insult this Lincoln despotism has put upon us?"

In August, two months after Baker's execution and in the same month Stephens's article appeared in the *Anglo-African*, there was a breakthrough. Attorney General Edward Bates ruled, with Lincoln's approval, that the Militia Act of 1862 requiring unequal pay didn't apply to soldiers who were freed before the start of the war. Few of the men of the Fifty-Fourth but many from the Fifty-Fifth had been slaves at the start of the war. Colonel Hallowell devised a "Quaker oath" for African American soldiers to pledge: "that no man had the right to demand unrequited labor [work without pay] of you, so help you God."

In September of 1864, one month after Gooding's death, Massachusetts Black regiments received twenty months' back pay of $13 per month for a total of $260 per soldier, or $260,000 per regiment—more than half a million dollars for the two regiments!

Ellen Gooding, the widow of a man who had died without pay, received James Henry Gooding's money. Soldiers walking up to the paymaster's table on September 28 imagined their families' surprise and joy when the money arrived. One soldier of the Fifty-Fourth composed a song that filled the night air around the campfires:

> *Fight we like men our conflict,*
> *Renew our vows to-night,*
> *For God and for our Country,*
> *For Freedom and the Right.*

Stephens, who joined the army in April 1863, went seventeen months without being able to send money home to his family. This left his wife, children, and mother-in-law dependent on charity, and it stung his pride and left him feeling tricked. But thousands of Black soldiers fighting and dying for the Union while refusing to be paid forced the federal government to give in to their protest, which Stephens supported with his words and deeds. Yet he wrote not a word about the Fifty-Fourth's greatest victory, *equal pay*. Neither did he praise Abraham Lincoln for correcting a wrong, nor criticize him for taking too long to correct an injustice. Even when Colonel James Montgomery resigned and returned to Kansas, Stephens withheld his pen. He had promised readers he would keep protesting the army's wrongs: "nothing shall prevent me but double irons or a pistol-ball that shall take me out of the hell I am now suffering." But after his published report of September 17, 1864, there were no more articles. He stopped writing for the *Anglo-African*.

Stephens and the Fifty-Fourth had won, at great cost, but Stephens wasn't finished fighting. Criticizing the army, its officers, or Abraham Lincoln, the commander-in-chief, wasn't enough. He wanted to be an officer in the U.S. Army. Officers were paid $105 a month, but more than the money, being a lieutenant meant that his bravery, ability, work habits, and most of all his intelligence would be recognized. As slavery's days neared an end, Stephens was ready for the war that still needed to be fought—the idea that there was a relationship between skin color and intelligence. Race prejudice, the other war, would last much longer than slavery.

CHAPTER FIFTEEN

THE OTHER WAR

On February 18, 1865, proud Charleston fell with an earth-rattling *boom*, louder and deadlier than any noise Stephens had ever heard. The sound and force startled him as he stood guard on a harbor island outpost. His mind raced to casualties: How many? Union or Confederate? And what kind of artillery shell could shake the ground for miles around and billow smoke out over the islands?

The massive detonation had been an accident, the result of a hasty and careless Confederate retreat. The last months of 1864 favored the Union. Abraham Lincoln was reelected and General William Tecumseh Sherman's Union forces burned their way across Georgia, leaving Atlanta in flames and capturing the port of Savannah.

Charleston lay just 100 miles up the coast, within Sherman's sights. Charleston's residents panicked. The city had already been under siege by Union artillery for more than a year, and whole sections were burned out or reduced to rubble. With Sherman's

Union Army headed in their direction, residents began to flee. The Confederate Army also packed its bags and abandoned Charleston. They spiked cannons, burned equipment, scuttled boats and warships, destroyed storehouses of cotton and rice, and stripped the city of its defenses and supplies before departing.

Half-forgotten by the fleeing army was a cache of foodstuffs and gunpowder at the Northeastern Railroad depot. In their rush to leave, soldiers had taken most of the food but not the gunpowder. As soon as they departed, women and children scurried through the depot, picking through the building for any food left behind. Children entertained themselves with found matches and lit scattered grains of black powder, giggling at the sight and sound of hissing sparks. When the sparkling fizzled out, another match was struck, and another—until the sparkler snaked into the powder room. The blast set off a hurricane of flying shrapnel, splintered bricks, and chunks of mortar. More than 200 died—more civilian deaths than Charleston had suffered in four years of war.

When Stephens learned of this self-inflicted wound, he knew the war was over for Charleston. At last Stephens would return to the city where eight years earlier he had been jailed and almost sold at a slave auction.

On February 18, 1865, Stephens and a squad from B Company crossed over to Morris Island and then rowed to Charleston. They became "the first effective force to actually take possession of the modern Babylon." Stephens compared the fallen city to a biblical town known as a place of sin and pride. That afternoon the Twenty-First United States Colored Troops, many of whom were once Charleston slaves, marched into Charleston followed later by men of the Massachusetts Fifty-Fifth—to the joy and almost disbelief of the crowds of African Americans who greeted them. The full regiment of the Fifty-Fourth marched into Charleston a week later.

While in the city Stephens searched for the men captured at Fort Wagner and imprisoned in the city jail. His B Company's detachment hurried down Magazine Street to the four-story jail, hidden behind a high wall. They broke open the unguarded doors but found only rats inside. White criminals had been released, and Black prisoners of war had been carried off with the retreating rebel army.

Out of curiosity they went to Ryan's Mart, the principal slave market in Charleston. Tucked in the center of the city, the "Mart," also known as "Ryan's nigger-jail," was where slave traders called themselves "brokers" and their business "black ivory." The Mart was just one of twenty-six Charleston slave auction houses that did a $16-million-a-year business.

The Mart was actually two houses joined together, each four stories high, where the enslaved were kept in locked cells until auction day. A morgue, or "dead room," stood nearby. In the large auction gallery, a cobwebbed platform stood like a stage empty of actors. From this platform thousands of men, women, and children had been displayed like farm animals at a state fair, while bidders inspected, prodded, and tried to outbid each other.

Stephens inhaled the odor of stale sweat ripened in southern humidity; the smell of fear and despair still clung to the walls. Shaken by his surroundings, Stephens could only be reminded of his father's stories of slavery and revolt, and the randomness of his own luck. Stephens himself might easily have landed on this very auction block eight years ago, had his ship's officer not rescued him. Or he might have landed here had his White grandfather not freed Stephens's father, or if Stephens's parents had not been wise enough to leave Virginia when they did. All those actions had made it possible for him to become Sergeant Stephens of the Union Army, something his parents applauded and his grandfathers would have scorned.

Confederate general Robert E. Lee, who said he would "rather die a thousand deaths" than surrender, finally met with Union general Ulysses S. Grant, and on April 9, 1865, surrendered his Army of Northern Virginia.

Some 350 miles south of Lee and Grant's meeting, Stephens

was one of 2,500 soldiers with no knowledge the war was over. Trekking across the South Carolina countryside, they were part of three Union brigades searching for Confederate trains. Along the way they broke up railroad tracks, disabled locomotives, and burned train cars and railroad equipment. And they shot at gray-coated soldiers who, also not knowing the war had ended, shot back.

But on the evening of April 22, the Fifty-Fourth gathered in a field to cheer and fire their rifles in celebration of the just-received news. Lee had surrendered two weeks earlier. Their exultation was short-lived, however, for the next day they learned that John Wilkes Booth had murdered Abraham Lincoln. Lieutenant-Colonel Hooper, who had led the Fifty-Fourth's retreat at Olustee, described the regiment's shock: "at first we could not comprehend it, it was too overwhelming, too lamentable, too distressing. We said quietly, 'Now there is *no more* peace, let us turn back, again load our muskets and if necessary, exterminate the race that can do such things . . .' Thus we all felt."

A freed slave felt the same despair: "The rebs won't let us alone. If they can't kill us, they'll kill all our frien's."

By the time the Fifty-Fourth received news of Lincoln's assassination, the president's red, white, and blue funeral train

John Wilkes Booth, an actor and Confederate zealot, shot Abraham Lincoln on April 14, 1865. He was caught and killed on April 26, 1865.

Carrying father and son, the train made 170 stops and traveled through seven states. Thousands stood in silence to pay their respects as the train passed through their towns on its way to Springfield, Illinois, for Lincoln's and his son's burial.

had already left Washington. On board, in two ice-packed caskets, were Lincoln and his eleven-year-old son Willie, who had died of typhoid fever during Lincoln's second year as president and would be re-interred with his father.

The train stopped in Philadelphia, where Stephens's family lived. Three quarters of a million mourners filed past the flag-draped casket in Independence Hall, where the Declaration of Independence and U.S. Constitution had been signed.

The next day, in the once-Confederate-leaning New York City, the president's body lay in state at City Hall. When the viewing was over, 85,000 mourners, including 2,000 African Americans, marched behind the hearse as it traveled to the Hudson River Station. From there, the slain president and his son continued their solemn journey to Springfield, Illinois, where they would be buried.

African Americans with bowed heads and shattered hearts stood alongside railroad tracks from Washington, DC, to Springfield, Illinois, to catch a glimpse of Lincoln's funeral train. They came to honor the president who had slowly come to understand that "without slavery the rebellion could never have existed; without slavery it could not continue." And they feared for their future.

Stephens left no record of his reaction to the loss of Abraham Lincoln, or his thoughts about the vice president, Andrew Johnson, who became the seventeenth president of the United States. We can only speculate that although Stephens disagreed with Lincoln's slow movement on slavery and unfair treatment of African American soldiers, there can be no doubt he feared the damage that President Andrew Johnson could cause in the fight for racial equality. Johnson, a former slaveholder, had proudly declared:

> I have lived among negroes, all my life, and I am
> for this Government with slavery under the
> Constitution as it is . . . I am for the Government of my
> fathers with negroes. I am for it without negroes.
> Before I would see this Government destroyed,
> I would send every negro back to Africa, disintegrated
> and blotted out of space.

For Stephens, no matter how skeptical he had been of Abraham Lincoln, Andrew Johnson meant that the other war—the battle against racial arrogance that demanded unequal treatment based on skin color—would continue even after slavery was dead.

CHAPTER SIXTEEN

A FINAL FIGHT AND MUSTERING OUT

The battle against the "iron hand of prejudice" continued. Stephens worked to become an officer. Promotion was second only to equal pay, and his hopes brightened when Colonel Hallowell recommended Sergeant Major Stephen Swails to become a lieutenant.

Swails had risked his life trying to help Captains Russel and Simpkins, two young officers who died together at Wagner. Swails had also been wounded at Olustee while delivering battlefield reports to Hallowell. After recovering, Swails returned to duty, and in March 1864, Hallowell recommended him for a promotion. Without delay, Massachusetts governor Andrew approved the promotion, and Swails, in his officer's straps, assumed his new duties without waiting for the War Department's routine approval. But "[w]hen the usual request was made, it was refused on account of Lieutenant Swails's African descent, although to all appearances he was a white man," and he was ordered to "take duty as an enlisted man."

Hallowell and Swails lobbied for nine months before his commission was approved. It required the sergeant major to travel to the Union's Department of the South headquarters in Hilton Head where, upon seeing Swails's near-white complexion, the reviewing officers approved his promotion. In January 1865, he became Second Lieutenant Swails and the first African American officer promoted by the U.S. Army.

Stephens also expected to be promoted. And during the winter of 1864, while stationed in Charleston, he took on more officer-like clerical duties. When not on guard duty he wrote reports. Colonel Hallowell had no one better qualified to handle the information required now that the war was ending. Stephens spent his days not only writing but also making sure there was a smooth flow of reports between the regiment, the Department of the South at Hilton Head, and the War Department in Washington, DC.

Stephens chose not to be the loud outspoken critic. In the fall of 1864 he had stopped complaining about Abraham Lincoln or writing about his own loss of patriotism. He would do nothing more to harm his chances of becoming an officer, and in July of 1865 his efforts paid off. Hallowell, now a general, recommended Stephens to become a second lieutenant. For Stephens it was, at last, recognition of his abilities on and off the battlefield.

Two other African American sergeants from the Fifty-Fourth, Peter Vogelsang and Frank Welch, were also recommended to be second lieutenants. The governor and the War Department approved their promotions. Of the regiment's twenty-four officers, three were now African Americans. Stephens expected he would be the fourth. Lieutenants Swails, Vogelsang, and Welch had near-white complexions while Stephens was slightly darker. Governor Andrew approved Stephens's promotion but the War Department rejected it "because of Stephens's race."

A few days later, he learned the Fifty-Fourth would return to Boston where they would be mustered out.

From Elmira, New York, the 31-year-old Swails replaced Lewis Douglass as the Fifty-Fourth's sergeant major and was wounded at the Battle of Olustee. After a long struggle with the War Department, Swails became the first African American officer commissioned by the U.S. Army.

On Saturday morning, September 2, 1865, as the sun settled high over Boston, the Fifty-Fourth Massachusetts Infantry victoriously marched from Commercial Wharf to the Boston Common. They had waited five days on Gallops Island in the Boston Harbor, where they turned in equipment, filled out papers, and received their final pay. One island away, the prisoner of war Alexander Hamilton Stephens sat locked in his cell. He experienced the same feelings that George E. Stephens had felt inside a Charleston cell eight years earlier for being a free African American sailor from the North. From George's Island, in the Boston Harbor, the Confederate vice president bemoaned his arrest and isolation: "The horrors of imprisonment, close confinement, no one to see or talk to, with the reflection of being cut off for I know not how long and perhaps forever—from communication with dear ones at home, are beyond description. Words utterly fail to express the soul's anguish."

While one Stephens languished in a prison fort, the other Stephens marched triumphantly into the city. Ever defiant, George E. Stephens ignored the War Department's rejection of his promotion and paraded with lieutenant's shoulder straps on his jacket. Thousands of Black and White cheering spectators welcomed him and the Fifty-Fourth home. The color guard carried the tattered, bullet-riddled Massachusetts and American flags, and the soldiers stepped to the band music with pride that came from knowing they had erased all doubts that African Americans would stand and fight to protect their country, even when that country refused to accept them as equal citizens.

Colonel Kurtz and his policemen marched alongside the regiment, just as they had when the soldiers departed for South Carolina in May of 1863. On this march, however, there were no rumors of a mob attack, and the stuffy businessmen at the Somerset Club did not lower their shades to shun the returning Fifty-Fourth. The Civil War had been won, and everyone welcomed the warriors home.

A reporter caught Boston's mood: "The Fifty-Fourth Massachusetts Regiment, the pioneer State colored regiment of this country . . . now returns crowned with laurels, and after two hundred thousand of their brethren . . . have fought themselves into public esteem."

Following the parade and a speech by Governor Andrew, Ned Hallowell thanked his men and praised their courage and sacrifice. With a regretful voice, the brigadier general dismissed the regiment for the last time. Twenty-four months of fighting the Confederacy in Georgia, South Carolina, and Florida ended with the last tap of the drum—and thirty months of fighting their own army for equal pay and rank ended on the last bugle note. Many of the men who marched out of Boston in 1863 and those who joined later did not return in 1865. Of the Fifty-Fourth's 1,354 men who served, 500 were either killed or wounded. Included among those were Corporal James Henry Gooding and Colonel Robert Gould Shaw.

Shaw's mother sent money to rebuild Darien, the town in

OMNIA RELINQVIT
SERVARE REMPVBLICAM

ROBERT GOVLD SHAW KILLED WHILE LEADING THE ASSAVLT ON FORT WAGNER JVLY TWENTY THIRD EIGHTEEN HVNDRED AND SIXTY THREE

Sculptor Augustus Saint-Gaudens's memorial to Robert Gould Shaw and his soldiers was erected in 1897. It honors the Black and White soldiers of the Fifty-Fourth Infantry and shows their departure from Boston Common on May 28, 1863.

Georgia that the Fifty-Fourth had burned. And Shaw's father declined to have his son's remains returned to Boston from the mass grave outside the walls of Fort Wagner. He spurned the offer: "We can imagine no holier place than that in which he lies, . . . nor wish for him better company." Their sandy graves have since washed into the stormy Atlantic Ocean—but not from history.

A bronze monument honoring Shaw and the men of the Fifty-Fourth who died at Fort Wagner now stands at the steps of the Boston Common, across the street from Massachusetts's gold-domed State House, where the soldiers had drilled on the day they left for South Carolina and war. Sailing to those battlefields, Shaw had written, "[I]f the raising of coloured troops prove such a benefit to the country, and to the blacks, as many people think it will, I shall thank God a thousand times that I was led to take my share in it."

Following the Fifty-Fourth's final parade, the New Bedford men of C Company returned home. Ellen Gooding and hundreds of other widows, wives, parents, and friends welcomed them. Ellen wore black in memory of her husband of six months who had fought at James Island, Fort Wagner, and Olustee without pay. Corporal James Henry Gooding served seventeen months with an unflinching belief that Black soldiers' willingness to die for the United States would persuade White Americans that Americans of African descent deserved the full rights, liberties, and freedoms of their country. Gooding and 65,000 African American soldiers threw themselves on an "Altar of the Nation" to "vindicate a foul aspersion that they were not men."

Stephens returned to Philadelphia. For twenty-three years, right up to his death on April 24, 1888, he continued to fight the War Department for his commission and officer's pay. Three years after his death, in 1891, the War Department reversed its decision and admitted that his promotion had been denied because of racial prejudice. Stephens was granted a posthumous U.S. Army commission.

On October 12, 1865, President Andrew Johnson pardoned former Confederate vice president Alexander Hamilton Stephens.

George E. Stephens, in one of his last wartime letters, mournfully wished: "Oh that this nation could learn wisdom by the lessons of the past!"

CHAPTER SEVENTEEN
FORWARD, MARCH!

Three months after the Fifty-Fourth mustered out of the army, American slavery legally ended. On December 6, 1865, the Thirteenth Amendment was ratified by enough states to outlaw the enslavement of humans in the United States.

Today it is hard to believe that a nation built on the principle of equality under the law required so many to die to decide if one human had the right to own another. At stake was the liberty of four million enslaved Americans. And like most great victories, it came at a dear price. Three months before the war started, George E. Stephens predicted, "A glorious destiny will be worked out for our people though millions of lives should have to pay the forfeiture." Four years later the country became painfully aware of the human cost. Ending "American slavery" claimed the lives of at least 315,000 Confederates, most of whom had never owned a slave, and as many as 435,000 Union lives, few of whom thought

Lincoln pushed for the Thirteenth Amendment, which would make slavery unconstitutional. Although his signature was not required, Lincoln knew this amendment would be one of his hallmark achievements, and he signed the amendment before it went to the states for ratification. Notice how Lincoln aged during the four years of war by comparing this photo with the one on page 23.

slaves were worth the sacrifice. But the men of the Fifty-Fourth never doubted that their actions would shape the future of the country their ancestors had helped build.

African Americans gave the Union Army a weapon the Confederates dared not use—Black soldiers. The Fifty-Fourth and

165 other African American regiments tipped the scale to victory and changed the presidency of Abraham Lincoln. Almost four years after the start of the war, and a few weeks after sending the Thirteenth Amendment to the states for ratification, Lincoln spoke of that change. American slavery had to end, he said, even if it meant that "every drop of blood drawn with the lash, shall be paid by another drawn with the sword."

In the spilling of that blood, 65,000 Black soldiers died in the two years they were in the war. And like Corporal James Henry Gooding, they fought to abolish slavery in *all* states, not to save a Union that would allow slavery in *some* states. Nearly 180,000 Black Americans served in the Union Army, and all of them, like Lieutenant George E. Stephens, fought to create a nation of equal citizens. Joining Gooding and Stephens in their battle against racial arrogance and privilege were thousands of Blacks and Whites whose courage and sense of duty nudged the nation forward.

That movement forward stumbled on Tuesday, April 11, 1865. Two days after the surrender of General Lee's army, the president stood at a window over the north portico of the White House. A rain-soaked crowd below cheered and demanded a victory speech. Instead Lincoln spoke of his plans to heal a reunited United States. It would be his last public speech. John Wilkes Booth, who was quietly mingling with the crowd, heard Lincoln say he favored giving some Blacks the vote, particularly "those who serve our cause as soldiers." Booth seethed, "That means nigger citizenship. Now, by God, I'll put him through."

Although it would take more than another hundred years for African Americans to gain full liberties as American citizens, neither John Wilkes Booth nor Alexander Hamilton Stephens could stop the ideas that George E. Stephens and James Henry Gooding fought for. May their stories never be forgotten.

SLAVERY AND CIVIL WAR

This 1864 campaign poster shows Abraham Lincoln and his running mate, Andrew Johnson. Following Abraham Lincoln's assassination, Johnson became the seventeenth president of the United States.

 "One eighth of the whole population were colored slaves, not distributed generally over the Union, but localized in the Southern part of it. These slaves constituted a peculiar and powerful interest. All knew that this interest was, somehow, the cause of the war."

Abraham Lincoln
Second Inaugural Address
March 4, 1865

 The Thirteenth Amendment outlawing slavery "in the United States, or any place subject to their jurisdiction" was ratified on December 6, 1865, eight months following Abraham Lincoln's assassination. After 246 years, American slavery was dead.

TIMELINE

1857

- Dred Scott decision: African Americans, because of their African heritage, are not American citizens.

1859

- George Stephens publishes his first article in the *Weekly Anglo-African*.
- John Brown's raid on the federal arsenal at Harpers Ferry, Virginia.
- John Brown is executed, and John Wilkes Booth, disguised as a federal soldier, is there to witness.

1860

- Abraham Lincoln is elected president.
- South Carolina secedes from the United States.

1861

- Mississippi, Florida, Alabama, Georgia, and Louisiana secede.
- Jefferson Davis becomes president of the Confederate States of America.
- Texas secedes.
- Abraham Lincoln is inaugurated as the sixteenth president of the United States.
- Civil War starts in Charleston, South Carolina.
- Virginia secedes.
- Arkansas and North Carolina secede.
- Kentucky, birth state of both Lincoln and Davis, proclaims its neutrality.
- Tennessee becomes the last state to secede.

1862

- Militia Act authorizes Blacks as army laborers, to be paid $10 a month, of which $3 can be withheld for clothing.
- Battle of Antietam (Maryland) in which Robert Gould Shaw fights.
- Abraham Lincoln announces the preliminary Emancipation Proclamation.

- Battle of Fredericksburg (Virginia) in which Stephens tells *Anglo-African* readers that the Union defeat means the Emancipation Proclamation is needed more than ever.
- Slavery in Washington, DC, is abolished.

1863

- Abraham Lincoln issues the Emancipation Proclamation, declaring slaves in seceding states free but not those in the four loyal slave states (Delaware, Maryland, Kentucky, and Missouri). The proclamation authorizes African Americans as soldiers in the Union Army but does not replace the Militia Act of 1862.
- War Department authorizes the Fifty-Fourth Regiment, "a special corps composed of persons of African descent." They are to receive the same pay as White soldiers.
- Henry Gooding's first article appears in the *New Bedford Mercury*.
- First volunteers of the Fifty-Fourth arrive at Camp Meigs, south of Boston.
- War Department establishes the Bureau of United States Colored Troops (USCT). By the end of the war there are 166 African American regiments in the Union Army. Massachusetts Fifty-Fourth and Fifty-Fifth are not under the authority of the USCT bureau. Massachusetts governor Andrew continues as their commander-in-chief.
- The Fifty-Fourth sails from Boston to Hilton Head, South Carolina.
- The Fifty-Fourth participates in the plundering and burning of Darien, Georgia.
- The Massachusetts Fifty-Fifth is formed with the overflow volunteers from the Fifty-Fourth.
- New York City Draft Riots.
- Boston Draft Riot.
- The Fifty-Fourth participates in its first battle and saves the Tenth Connecticut.
- The Fifty-Fourth leads the second attack on Fort Wagner on Morris Island, South Carolina, and suffers 279 casualties, including Colonel Robert Gould Shaw.

- Lincoln issues an Order of Retaliation against the Confederates.
- Frederick Douglass meets Abraham Lincoln, who promises equal pay for Black soldiers and the appointment of Black officers. No action occurs for eleven months.
- The Fifty-Fourth participates in the Union siege that forces Confederates' evacuation of Fort Wagner.
- Confederate general Patrick Cleburne proposes that slaves be trained as soldiers and those who fight be emancipated. President Jefferson Davis rejects the proposal.
- Corporal James Henry Gooding writes a letter to President Lincoln and asks, "Are we not soldiers?"

1864

- The Fifty-Fourth fights in the Battle of Olustee and suffers 66 casualties, including Corporal James Henry Gooding.
- Private Baker of the Fifty-Fifth is executed for striking an officer.
- Congress authorizes equal pay for Black soldiers.
- Gooding dies at Andersonville Prison.
- Lincoln is reelected president.
- Six companies of the Fifty-Fourth participate in the Battle of Honey Hill and suffer 39 casualties. Stephens is on duty at a different location and does not participate in this battle.
- Stephen Swails of the Fifty-Fourth is promoted to second lieutenant and becomes the first Black officer in the United States Army.

1865

- Lincoln delivers his second inaugural address.
- Confederate Congress, desperate for more soldiers, authorizes the use of slaves as soldiers. Jefferson Davis approves and Robert E. Lee declares it "not only expedient but necessary."
- General Robert E. Lee surrenders at Appomattox, Virginia.
- Lincoln speaks from a White House window and expresses support for giving Black soldiers the right to vote.
- John Wilkes Booth assassinates Lincoln.
- Andrew Johnson, a former slaveowner, becomes president of the United States.

- The Fifty-Fourth, unaware that Lee has surrendered or that Lincoln has been assassinated, fights in the Battle of Boykin's Mill and suffers 18 casualties.
- John Wilkes Booth is captured and killed.
- Jefferson Davis is captured in Irwinville, Georgia (near Andersonville), and imprisoned for two years in Virginia.
- Alexander Stephens is arrested at his home in Crawford, Georgia, and imprisoned for five months on an island in the Boston Harbor.
- Sergeant George E. Stephens's promotion to lieutenant is denied by the War Department because of his race.
- President Johnson declares the Civil War over. An estimated 750,000 Americans have died over the issue of Black slavery.
- The Emancipation Proclamation is read in Galveston, Texas, for the first time and begins the annual Juneteenth celebration that continues to this day.
- Booth's four co-conspirators are hanged (Mary Surratt, Lewis Powell, David Herold, and George Atzerodt).
- Henry Wirz, commander of Andersonville, is executed.
- The Fifty-Fourth's victory march in Boston. Stephens marches as a first lieutenant.
- Emancipation Ordinance of Missouri frees the author's maternal grandfather.
- Thirteenth Amendment is ratified, abolishing slavery and involuntary servitude.

1868
- Fourteenth Amendment is ratified, confirming that African Americans born in the United States are American citizens.

1870
- Fifteenth Amendment is ratified, affirming that no one can be denied the right to vote because of race, color, or former slave status.

1888
- George E. Stephens dies at age 56 (the same age as Lincoln at his death) in Brooklyn, New York.

1891

- Stephens's promotion is approved by the War Department and he is posthumously promoted to the rank of lieutenant.

1897

- The Shaw Memorial Monument, honoring the soldiers of the Fifty-Fourth who died at Fort Wagner, is unveiled on the Boston Common. It faces the Massachusetts State House, where Governor Andrew planned for a regiment of soldiers of African descent.

1900

- William Carney receives (in the mail) the Medal of Honor, the United States's highest military honor, for his valor beyond the call of duty. Although not awarded until 1900, it is for his action at Fort Wagner on July 18, 1863. He is one of 23 African Americans who fought in the Civil War to receive this honor.

SOURCE NOTES

The source of each quotation in this book appears below. The citation indicates the first few words of the quotation and its document source. The document sources appear in the bibliography that follows.

Frontispiece
"MEN OF COLOR . . ." Frederick Douglass's speech in Rochester, New York, on March 2, 1863

Chapter One—George E. Stephens
"throat of treason . . .": *Douglass's Monthly*, March 1863, p. 1
"Receive Me": Preble, p. 399
"upon the great truth . . .": Alexander H. Stephens, *Cornerstone Speech*
"Arouse, free black men! . . .": Yacovone, p. 125
"mixed blood": same as above, p. 3
"promising young . . .": same as above, p. 8
"a vigorous intellect . . .": same as above
"You must witness . . .": same as above, p. 10
"half clad, filthy . . .": same as above
"half-way house . . .": same as above
"Death lays his . . .": same as above, p. 11
"Why should we . . .": same as above, p. 120
"mouth-piece of . . .": same as above, p. 123
"[t]ake notice . . .": same as above
"[T]hat the negro . . .": same as above
"free able-bodied . . .": The Militia Act of 1792 (May 8, 1792), Section I

Chapter Two—Watch Night
"the men of . . .": Yacovone, pp. 138–39
"a posse of . . .": same as above, p. 133

128

"[I]t required 13 . . .": Yacovone, p. 133

"in full advance . . .": same as above, p. 208

"all negroes caught . . .": same as above, p. 209

"We could stand . . .": same as above, p. 213

"[t]he great battle . . .": same as above, pp. 210–11

"colored servants . . .": same as above, p. 215

"If military necessity . . .": same as above, p. 218

"This December 31st . . .": same as above

"necessitate a general . . .": same as above, p. 219

Chapter Three—James Henry Gooding

"of medium height . . .": Adams, p. xxii

"By virtue of . . .": Emancipation Proclamation

"And I further . . .": same as above

"forgo comfort, home . . .": Adams, p. 4

"[W]hen the slave . . .": same as above, p. 13

"mulatto": same as above, p. xxii

"a person of intelligence . . .": same as above, p. x

"And when far . . .": same as above, p. 131

"persons of African descent": Greennough, p. 30

"be a model . . .": Pearson, p. 74

"COLORED MEN . . .": recruitment handbill

"They do not . . .": Adams, p. 6

"Are the colored . . .": same as above, p. 4

"for honor, duty . . .": same as above, p. 14

"examined, sworn in . . .": Duncan (1), p. 304

"looking quite like . . .": Adams, p. 5

"Col. Shaw is . . .": same as above

"war of extermination": Duncan (1), p. 245

"Nigger Col.": same as above, p. 292

"The intelligence . . .": same as above, p. 313

"The glorious 54th . . .": Adams, p. 6

"negroes found with arms . . .": *Republican Standard*, January 1, 1863, p. 4

"There is not . . .": Adams, p. 24

Chapter Four—Call to Courage

"[w]e would be . . .": Yacovone, p. 231

"[A]ll attempts . . .": Nash, p. 232

"We don't want . . .": quoted in Smith (2), p. 6

"i would a little . . .": quoted in Yacovone, p. 27

"the whole and . . .": McCague, p. 11

"I do not exaggerate . . .": Yacovone, p. 235

"[T]hey intend us . . .": Adams, p. 16

"vindicate a foul . . ." same as above, p. 21

Chapter Five—Hope and Glory

"One Southern regiment . . .": Duncan (2), pp. 86–87

"Can we believe . . .": same as above, p. 85

"The fangs of . . .": Yacovone, p. 3

"The citizens of . . .": Adams, p. 24

"No white regiment . . .": quoted in Emilio, p. 33

"I John Brown . . .": Everhart, p. 60

"John Brown's body . . .": Brown, pp. 174–78

Chapter Six—I Shall Burn This Town

"How soon can . . .": Emilio, p. 40

"In half an . . .": same as above

"take twenty men . . .": Duncan (2), p. 94

"I shall burn . . .": same as above

"We are outlawed . . .": same as above, p. 343

"[o]ur active and . . .": Yacovone, p. 241

"When we left . . .": same as above, p. 242

"steamed gaily down . . .": same as above

"greeted the outbuildings . . .": same as above

"The first rebel . . .": same as above

"nigger guerillas": Duncan (2), p. 95

"cowardly Yankee negro . . .": same as above

"[I]nstead of improving . . .": same as above, pp. 94–95

"After our forces . . .": Adams, pp. 29–30

"Is there any . . .": Duncan (1), p. 362

"Then, be ready . . .": same as above

"I am the . . .": Yacovone, p. 298

"Our active . . ." same as above, p. 241

Chapter Seven—Paymaster's Wagon

"We are all . . .": Adams, p. 7

"TO COLORED MEN": recruitment broadside

"PAY, $13 . . .": same as above

"unjust in every . . .": McPherson (2), p. 203

"Do you think . . .": Blatt, p. 38

"Our enlistment itself . . .": Yacovone, p. 253

Chapter Eight—Dark Heroes

"Instead of going . . .": Adams, p. 32

"Is there no . . .": Yacovone, p. 240

"slowly and reluctantly . . .": same as above, p. 244

"The rebels yelled . . .": same as above

"Every man that . . .": same as above, p. 245

"The boys of . . .": Emilio, p. 60

"At last we . . .": Adams, p. 36

"nine killed, 13 . . .": same as above, p. 37

"dragged [him] through . . .": Spann, p. 99

"Kill the d—d nigger": same as above

"for fill[ing] the . . .": same as above, p. 102

"zeal for the . . .": same as above

"We wondered . . .": same as above, p. 38

Chapter Nine—A Grand Chance

"render[ed] the blackness . . .": Emilio, p. 64

"groping their way . . .": same as above, p. 65

"one of the . . .": Burchard (caption note), unnumbered signature
     after p. 77

"Well I guess . . .": Duncan (2), p. 110

"We were on . . .": Adams, p. 39

"grand chance . . .": Duncan (2), p. 110

"of the previous . . .": Yacovone, p. 245

"I am sorry . . .": Emilio, p. 77

"If this man . . .": same as above

"I will": same as above

"Move in quick . . .": same as above, p. 79

"Forward!": same as above

Chapter Ten—Dear Old Flag

"It was about . . .": Emilio, p. 79

"get at the throat . . .": Douglass Monthly, March 21, 1863, p. 1

"hailed by the civilized . . .": Preble, p. 418

"they mowed us . . .": Adams, p. 39

"Mortal men . . .": same as above, p. 38

"Come on, men . . .": Yacovone, p. 246

"When the men . . .": Adams, p. 39

"[T]hey, to a man, . . .": Yacovone, p. 246

"Thus we lost . . .": same as above

"skedaddling": same as above

"dear old flag": Burchard, p. 141

"stripped of all . . .": Emilio, p. 98

"Had he been . . .": same as above, p. 99

Chapter Eleven—Are We Soldiers?

"grand chance": Duncan (2), p. 110

"an ordinary spectacle . . .": Adams, p. 55

"mob-fiends . . .": Yacovone, p. 250

"*Mr. Editor*: Fort . . .": same as above, p. 264

"The smell in . . .": Adams, p. 58

"All who wished . . .": same as above, p. 48–49

"I am glad . . .": same as above, p. 48

"Too many of . . .": same above, p. 49

"insulting" and "about half the . . .": Yacovone, p. 277

"Your Excellency . . .": National Archives, Record Group No. 94, and Adams, p. 118

"Are we Soldiers . . .": same as above, p. 119

"the privilege of . . .": Gooding's letter to Lincoln

"I am your . . .": Yacovone, p. 278

"A great many . . .": same as above

"placed on the . . .": same as above

"worshipped snakes . . .": same as above

"Your features can . . .": same as above, p. 279

"mutiny is punishable . . .": same as above

"As to yellow . . .": same as above, p. 284

"avert it before . . .": Adams, p. 122

"[t]he African race . . .": same as above

"say a thousand . . .": same as above

"they may know . . .": same as above

"mistake in law . . .": same as above, p. 123

Chapter Twelve—Three Cheers
"[W]e were off . . .": Adams, p. 112

"no strenuous opposition . . .": same as above, p. 114

"to restore Florida . . .": Emilio, p. 148

"colored brigade": same as above, p. 162

"We're bound for . . .": same as above, p. 159

"That's home-made . . .": same as above, p. 162

"I don't mind . . .": same as above

"Three cheers for . . .": same as above, p. 163

"We're badly whipped!": same as above

"You'll all get . . .": same as above

"a stupendous ambuscade": Yacovone, p. 295

"The two colored . . .": Emilio, p. 167

"here to steal . . .": Nulty, p. 128

"Now, men, you . . .": Emilio, p. 168

"wooly head": Nulty, p. 211
"I tell you . . .": same as above, p. 211

Chapter Thirteen—Andersonville
"die in the . . .": McPherson, p. 792
"When the war . . .": Adams, p. 17
"a dozen . . .": Sneden, p. 225

Chapter Fourteen—Mutiny and Honor
"[M]oney or blood!": Blatt, p. 44
"[M]uster us out . . .": same as above
"white as a sheet . . .": Yacovone, p. 76
"under a tyranny . . .": same as above, p. 44
"I'm not going . . .": Yacovone, p. 46
"I won't do . . .": same as above
"You dammed white . . .": same as above
"For God's sake . . .": Yacovone, p. 75
"Nearly eighteen months . . .": same as above, p. 76
"that no man . . .": Blatt, p. 50
"Fight we like . . .": same as above, p. 51
"nothing shall prevent . . .": Yacovone, p. 76

Chapter Fifteen—The Other War
"the first effective . . .": Yacovone, p. 80
"Ryan's nigger-jail": Bancroft, p. 171
"rather die a . . .": Katcher, p. 182
"at first we . . .": Wickman, p. 26
"The rebs won't . . .": McPherson (2), p. 311
"without slavery the . . .": Basler Vol. V, p. 530
"I have lived . . .": Trefousse, p. 166

Chapter Sixteen—Returning Home
"iron hand of prejudice": New-England Anti-Slavery Convention,
    January 1834, p. 41

"[w]hen the usual . . .": Emilio, p. 194

"take duty as . . .": same as above

"because of his race": Yacovone, p. 90

"The horrors of . . .": Stephens, *Recollections*, p. 133

"The Fifty-fourth . . .": Emilio, p. 321

"We can imagine . . .": Foote, p. 120

"[I]f the raising . . .": Duncan (1), p. 335

"Altar of the Nation": Adams, p. 119

"vindicate a foul . . .": same as above, p. 21

"Oh that this . . .": Yacovone, p. 323

Chapter Seventeen—Forward, March!

"A glorious destiny . . .": Yacovone, p. 127

"American slavery": Basler Vol. VIII, p. 333

"every drop of . . .": same as above

"those who serve . . .": same as above, p. 403

"That means nigger . . .": Kauffman, p. 210

Slavery and Civil War

"One eighth of . . .": Basler Vol. VIII, p. 332

Timeline

"a special corps . . .": Emilio, p. 2

"not only expedient . . .": Levine, p. 5

BIBLIOGRAPHY

Now or Never: Fifty-Fourth Massachusetts Infantry's War to End Slavery is woven from confirmed facts, and the story behind those facts. It is essentially the story of two African American soldiers who answered Abraham Lincoln's call to save the Union and liberate slaves—their hopes, fears, flaws, and sacrifices as they struggled against the nation's then-accepted social and legal race-based restrictions. It is also the story of Colonel Robert Gould Shaw, the man these two soldiers served under. In telling the stories of Gooding, Stephens, and Shaw, I have relied on the research and transcriptions of three scholars whose works made this book possible: Donald A. Yacovone's *A Voice of Thunder: The Civil War Letters of George E. Stephens*; Virginia M. Adams's *On the Altar of Freedom: A Black Soldier's Civil War Letters from the Front*; and Russell Duncan's *Blue-Eyed Child of Fortune: The Civil War Letters of Colonel Robert Gould Shaw*.

NEWSPAPERS

Anglo-African

Boston Commonwealth

Boston Pilot

Charleston Mercury

Douglass's Monthly

New Bedford Mercury

New York Daily Tribune

Republican Standard

Savannah Daily Morning News

BOOKS

Adams, Virginia Matzke, ed. *On the Altar of Freedom: A Black Soldier's Civil War Letters from the Front*. Amherst: University of Massachusetts Press, 1992.

Andrew, William L., ed. *The Oxford Frederick Douglass Reader*. New York: Oxford University Press, 1996.

Bancroft, Frederic. *Slave Trading in the Old South*. Columbia, SC: University of South Carolina Press, 1996.

Basler, Roy P., ed. *Collected Works: The Abraham Lincoln Association, Springfield, Illinois*. Vols. VI–VII. New Brunswick, NJ: Rutgers University Press, 1953.

Blatt, Martin H., Thomas J. Brown, and Donald Yacovone, eds. *Hope & Glory: Essays on the Legacy of the Fifty-Fourth Massachusetts Regiment*. Amherst, MA: University of Massachusetts Press, 2001.

Brown, C. A. (revised by Heaps, Willard.) *The Story of Our National Ballads*. New York: Hard Press, 1960.

Burchard, Peter. *One Gallant Rush*. New York: St. Martin's Press, 1965.

Burkett, Christopher. *50 Core American Documents: Required Reading for Students, Teachers, and Citizens*. Ashland, OH: Ashbrook Press, 2014.

Duncan, Russell. *Where Death and Glory Meet: Colonel Robert Gould Shaw and the 54th Massachusetts Infantry*. Athens, GA: University of Georgia Press, 1999.

Duncan, Russell, ed. *Blue-Eyed Child of Fortune: The Civil War Letters of Colonel Robert Gould Shaw*. Athens, GA: University of Georgia Press, 1992.

Emilio, Luis F. *A Brave Black Regiment: The History of the 54th Regiment of Massachusetts Volunteer Infantry, 1863–1865*. New York: Da Capo Press, 1995.

Everhart, William C., and Arthur L. Sullivan. *John Brown's Raid*. Washington, DC: National Park Service, 1974.

Foner, Philip S., ed. *Frederick Douglass: Selected Speeches and Writings*. Chicago: Lawrence Hill Books, 1999.

Foote, Lorien. *Seeking the One Great Remedy: Francis George Shaw and Nineteenth-Century Reform*. Athens, OH: Ohio University Press, 2003.

Glatthaar, Joseph T. *Forged in Battle: The Civil War Alliance of Black Soldiers and White Officers*. Baton Rouge: Louisiana State University Press, 2000.

Greennough, Sarah, and Nancy K. Anderson. *Tell It With Pride: The 54th Massachusetts Regiment and Augustus Saint-Gaudens' Shaw Memorial*. New Haven, CT: Yale University Press, 2013.

Katcher, Philip. *The Civil War Day by Day*. St. Paul, MN: Zenith Press, 2007.

McCague, James. *The Second Rebellion: The Story of the New York City Draft Riots of 1863*. New York: Dial Press, 1968.

McPherson, James M. *Tried by War: Abraham Lincoln as Commander in Chief*. New York: Penguin Press, 2008.

———. *The Negro's Civil War: How American Blacks Felt and Acted During the War for the Union*. New York: Vintage Books, 2003.

Militia Act of 1792. http://www.constitution.org/mil/mil_act_1792.htm.

Nash, Gary B. *First City: Philadelphia and the Forging of Historical Memory*. Philadelphia: University of Pennsylvania Press, 2002.

Nulty, William H. *Confederate Florida: The Road to Olustee*.

Tuscaloosa, AL: University of Alabama Press, 1990.

Pearson, Henry Greenleaf. *The Life of John A. Andrew, Governor of Massachusetts, 1861–1865*. Volume II. Boston: Houghton Mifflin, 1904.

Preble, George Henry. *Our Flag: Origin and Progress of the Flag of the United States of America*. Albany, NY: J. Munsell, 1872.

Proceedings of the New-England Anti-Slavery Convention. Boston: Garrison & Knapp, 1834.

Rintels, David W. *Andersonville: The Complete Original Screenplay*. Introduction by James McPherson. Baton Rouge: Louisiana State University Press, 1996.

Smith, John David (1). *Black Soldiers in Blue: African American Troops in the Civil War Era*. Chapel Hill, NC: University of North Carolina Press, 2002.

Smith, John David (2). *Lincoln and the U.S. Colored Troops*. Carbondale, IL: Southern Illinois University Press, 2013.

Sneden, Robert Knox. *Eye of the Storm: A Civil War Odyssey*. New York: Free Press, 2000.

Spann, Edward K. *Gotham at War: New York City, 1860–1865*. Lanham, MD: Rowman & Littlefield, 2002.

Stephens, Alexander H. *Recollections*. Baton Rouge, Louisiana State University Press, 1998 (1910).

Trefousse, Hans L. *Andrew Johnson: A Biography*. New York: W. W. Norton, 1989.

Von Abele, Rudolph. *Alexander H. Stephens: A Biography*. New York: Knopf, 1946.

Wakelyn, Jon, ed. *Southern Pamphlets on Secession, November 1860–April 1861*. Chapel Hill, NC: University of North Carolina Press, 1996.

Wickman, Don. "Their Share of Glory." *Rutland History Society Quarterly*, Vol. 22 No. 2, 1992.

Yacovone, Donald, ed. *A Voice of Thunder: The Civil War Letters of George E. Stephens*. Urbana, IL: University of Illinois Press, 1997.

FOR MORE INFORMATION

Bartoletti, Susan Campbell. *They Called Themselves the KKK: The Birth of an American Terrorist Group*. Boston: Houghton Mifflin Harcourt, 2010.

Bolden, Tonya. *Emancipation Proclamation: Lincoln and the Dawn of Liberty*. New York: Abrams, 2013.

Fleming, Candace. *The Lincolns: A Scrapbook Look at Abraham and Mary*. New York: Schwartz & Wade Books, 2008.

Freedman, Russell. *Abraham Lincoln and Frederick Douglass: The Story Behind an American Friendship*. Boston: Houghton Mifflin Harcourt, 2012.

Haskins, Jim, ed. *Black Stars of Civil War Times: African Americans Who Lived Their Dreams*. New York: Wiley & Sons, 2003.

Holzer, Harold. *Lincoln: How Abraham Lincoln Ended Slavery in America*. New York: Newmarket Press, 2012.

McPherson, James M. *Fields of Fury: The American Civil War*. New York: Atheneum, 2002.

ACKNOWLEDGMENTS

Although writing is lonely work, no writer works alone. I am grateful for the advice of Dr. John David Smith, the Charles H. Stone Distinguished Professor of American History at the University of North Carolina at Charlotte (any factual errors are this author's own), as well as the student reviewers in Daniel Weaver's publishing class at Emerson College. I am equally grateful for the photo research of Debbie Needleman and Raquel Sousa. I am also deeply indebted to the firm and guiding hand of Carolyn P. Yoder at Calkins Creek. And a special thanks goes to my good friend Marlowe Teig, who never grew tired of hearing me talk about this project, and to my writing colleagues, who understand the amount of shoe leather and seat time required for even this modest work: Mimsy Beckwith, Jim Chapman, David Cottingham, Martin Quitt, Frankie Wright, and the Boston Biographers Group. Thank you all!

Ray Anthony Shepard's maternal grandfather, Anthony Jackson (1859–1939), was born into slavery on a Missouri hemp farm in a part of the state known as Little Dixie. Jackson was declared free at the age of six with the passage of the Emancipation Ordinance of Missouri of January 11, 1865, two years after Abraham Lincoln's Emancipation Proclamation.

INDEX

Page numbers in **boldface** refer to images and/or captions.

PICTURE CREDITS